The Secret to Using Your Body

A Manual for Looking Better and Feeling Younger with the Alexander Technique

Leland Vall
AmSAT Certified Alexander Technique Instructor

The Secret to Using Your Body
A Manual for Looking Better and Feeling Younger with
the Alexander Technique
© 2010 Leland Vall All rights reserved.
www.freeyourneck.com
leland@freeyourneck.com

This book is designed to provide information in regard to the subject matter covered for healthy adults. It is sold with the understanding that the author is not rendering medical advice or other professional services. It is highly recommended that an examination by a physician be performed before attempting to begin any program outlined in this book.

The purpose of this book is to educate and to expand thinking about posture as an informational source for readers, and it is not medical advice, nor has it been evaluated by the FDA. The author shall have neither liability nor responsibility to any person or entity with respect to any loss or damage caused or alleged to be caused directly or indirectly by the information and programs contained in this book.

ISBN: 978-0-578-04485-9

Published by Leland Vall

Contents

Introduction

During my freshman year of college, I went to an introductory workshop on the Alexander Technique. I had heard about the Alexander Technique from an older cousin who described it vaguely as a method for finding happiness by improving posture. I didn't have any particular reason to go—my posture seemed fine to me—but I was curious.

When the class started there were about thirty people sitting in chairs in a circle. The instructor spoke for a few minutes about the limits of our self-perception, and then he went fairly quickly from person to person, gently but precisely touching and slightly moving each participant's head. I was sitting on the far end from where the instructor started and, as he worked with each person, it seemed to me that most of them changed a little. They seemed to become more at ease, and they smiled. When the instructor came to me, he gently held my head with both hands while slightly changing its position. The result was nothing short of an epiphany.

Immediately I felt as if I were being introduced to a new body. My head felt lighter and my torso seemed longer and wider. It was as if a pressing force that I hadn't been aware of was suddenly lifted from my body. I thought a secret about myself had been revealed to me and that maybe I was experiencing myself as I had when I was a child.

He had only moved my head a little bit but I knew it was more than that. At that moment I realized that at some point in the distant past, I had made an unconscious decision about how to hold my head that caused a background of discomfort I considered normal. I also realized that if I had made an unconscious decision about something so simple as how I held my head, it was likely that much of how I experienced myself was also based on countless similar decisions. In that one moment I understood that here was a method to help me rediscover my truer self. I was fascinated, and I have benefited from my study of the Alexander Technique ever since.

With this book you too can learn how to look and feel younger for the rest of your life, whether or not you exercise and regardless of your age or almost any physical condition. You can uncover secrets about yourself that will help you gain a renewed feeling of lightness, ease of movement, and improved posture, breathing, poise, and strength.

What is the Alexander Technique?

The Alexander Technique is a proven, 100-year-old method for developing a specific type of self-awareness that allows you to evaluate and improve the way you use your body. F. M. Alexander (1869–1955) recognized that people tend to use their bodies in a haphazard, inefficient way. Alexander developed what can be described as a set of instructions that help you discover how to use your body in a more organized way that takes advantage of our unique upright structure. Alexander's method is different from trying to stand up straight, which is difficult to maintain and tends to increase tension. It is also different from relaxation techniques, which do not address how to remain relaxed during normal activities like reaching, bending, and carrying.

The Secret to Using Your Body is a workbook that uses a daily 15–30 minute experiential exercise to teach you the fundamental principles of the Alexander Technique, step by step. Use the book on your own or as a supplement to lessons with a teacher. The book is narrow in scope and I have tried to include only the information that you need to make progress toward your goal. Step by step, as you learn the exercise, you will gain a clearer understanding of your body that will lead to an improvement in the way you use your body. Your posture will improve, you will feel lighter and taller, and you will move more easily. Once you learn the whole exercise, you can continue to use and benefit from it, and you will also be able to tailor the exercise to suit your needs. Over time, through practicing the full exercise, your understanding of how to use your body will become second nature, making the improvement permanent.

How to Benefit from the Exercise

The exercise is divided into ten major parts and further divided into forty-three short sections. Each section is only a few sentences long. **It is designed to be learned and practiced over time with each new section teaching you more of the Alexander Technique.** To begin, read through Section 1 and then practice it from memory as best you can. Repeat the same procedure every time you practice Section 1 until you feel that you know what you are asked to do. You only need to remember the ideas, you don't need to memorize the exercise word for word.

Learning the rest of the exercise is a process of continuing to practice what you know as you learn each new section. When you are ready to learn Section 2, read through it and then, from memory, practice both Sections 1 and 2 together. Continue practicing what you know and learning new sections until you are practicing the entire exercise. **The repetition of regularly practicing the exercise from the beginning deepens your understanding and helps you to assimilate what you are learning.**

Amount of Time Required

It could take several months or more to learn the whole exercise, but you can benefit from each step beginning today. For best results, spend 15–30 minutes learning and practicing the exercise every day. But even if you are short on time, use whatever time you have to practice as much as you can. It is better to spend even a little time than to skip a day, but you will find that more time is better than less.

When you begin, use the whole 15–30 minutes to read and practice Section 1. **As you add Section 2 and other sections, the amount of time you spend does not need to increase.** As the number of sections increases, you will spend less time with each individual section and the sections will begin to flow together. However, you can spend more time practicing the exercise if you want and you can also practice the exercise more than once per day.

Tips for Success

- Approach the exercise in a simple, enjoyable way. Don't think of it as a burden or something that you have to do.

- Practice the exercise every day, even if you only have a few minutes. For best results, spend 15–30 minutes.

- Avoid trying to get it perfectly right. Simply taking the time every day to practice the exercise is valuable in itself, and what you are able to learn will change and grow as you consistently take that time.

- The value of any given section may not be clear when you first encounter it, but the exercise will become clearer as you go. Every part and section is designed to help you discover a specific type of self-awareness that, when combined in the full exercise, will give you a new, integrated way of understanding your body.

- Be patient and remain open to new experiences, even if they are slow in coming. An analogy is walking into a quiet area and then noticing after a while that there are lots of little noises and things going on. The more you look and listen, the more you will find.

- Put the book aside while practicing the exercise and practice it as best you can from memory. You can make progress every time you practice the exercise, no matter how many days it takes to learn each new section.

- Follow the instructions to use your imagination or to "think as though" something were true.

- Do not work at applying the instructions to your daily life until you have finished learning the whole exercise. Avoid thinking "this is how I am supposed to" stand or move or bend.

I hope you enjoy the journey.

Part I
Lying Down

Before You Begin

Your body is more internally spacious than you think, and you can learn to have access to that extra space. People tend to draw their body inward, making the body shorter and narrower. In the exercise you will be asked to focus on allowing your body to be more open. Although this part of the exercise is performed lying down, it will give you insight into finding this same room within your body as you are asked to stand and move. Allowing for more internal space, even a very small increase, can have many benefits. These benefits can include looking taller and more confident, a general feeling of comfort with improved ease of movement, and more room for internal organs, which can lower blood pressure and improve breathing.

In this first part of the exercise you will lie on a mat or rug in a purposeful way. **The goal of this, and all the other parts of the exercise, is to help you develop the skill of allowing for more room within your body.** Perform the exercise by lying on your back with your head on a book as shown below. Leave your knees up and your feet flat on the floor. Leave your legs separate from each other so that they do not touch. Place your hands on your abdomen but do not let your fingers touch.

You can be comfortable, but not so comfortable that you begin to fall asleep. Think of this time you spend as an activity. Leave your eyes open and let your mind stay active and gently focused on the exercise. You will be resting because you will be lying down, so there is no need to work at resting. Don't rush. Give yourself plenty of time to repeat and understand each instruction every time.

Spend 15–30 minutes on the exercise every day. This first part of the exercise has eleven sections which you combine as you learn. As you practice the exercise, you may discover a subtle difference in how you experience your body. Try to remain open to new discoveries every time you do the exercise.

When you are ready to stand up, do it slowly and easily. Be aware of your surroundings and leave the exercise until the next time you practice it.

Equipment

You will need a mat or rug to lie on (something comfortable but firm) and a soft-cover book on which to place your head. You can put a towel over the book if you want. A pillow is too soft. If your torso is very thick or bent, you can use a stack of books. Your feet can be bare or you can wear shoes as long as your feet are not able to slide on the floor.

www.freeyourneck.com   5

This is the first section of the first part of the exercise. It may seem simple but it is important because it is the beginning and it sets up the foundation for the whole exercise. Take 15–30 minutes to read through pages 6 and 7 and then practice Section 1 from memory as best you can. Repeat this procedure every day until you feel ready to add Section 2 on page 8. Continue this process throughout the book to learn the whole exercise.

Part I, Section 1. Allow Yourself to Settle

Lie on your back with your head on the book, your feet flat on the floor (knees bent) and your hands on your abdomen. Imagine that you are almost weightless. Keep your hands apart and your knees separate from each other. Avoid moving around in order to look for the best position. Without pushing, allow your whole body to settle toward the floor (there will be some gaps between your back and the floor). Leave your eyes open.

When you are ready to stand up, do it slowly and easily. Be aware of your surroundings and leave the exercise until the next time.

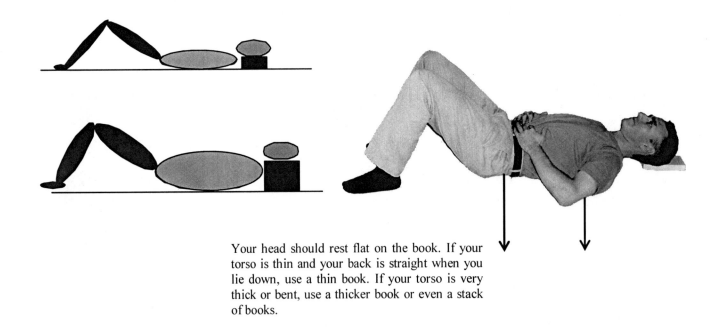

Your head should rest flat on the book. If your torso is thin and your back is straight when you lie down, use a thin book. If your torso is very thick or bent, use a thicker book or even a stack of books.

Remain open to new discoveries every time you practice the exercise.	Don't rush. Give yourself plenty of time to repeat and understand each instruction.	Look for comfort by waiting for your muscles to soften, not through shifting.

Sometimes, Doing a Little Less

"Allow" is a word that appears in the exercise many times. It means to continue doing less even when you think there is nothing less you can do.

Not Moving

Move if you have to, but try to avoid fidgeting.

Leaving Your Eyes Open

Stay awake. During the exercise, as you become more aware of yourself, continue to be aware of your surroundings.

Imagining Yourself Almost Weightless

You are not lying down just to rest. Imagining that you are effortlessly standing up gives you an objective beyond what you are doing now and will help you later in the exercise.

*When you have learned Section 1, add the new **bold** section to your practice and work on it just as you worked on the first section. Start from the beginning of the exercise every time and continue this process throughout the book. The amount of time you spend does not need to increase as you add more sections.*

Part I, Section 2. Allow Your Head to Release from the Top of Your Spine

Lie on your back with your head on the book, your feet flat on the floor (knees bent) and your hands on your abdomen. Imagine that you are almost weightless. Keep your hands apart and your knees separate from each other. Avoid moving around in order to look for the best position. Without pushing, allow your whole body to settle toward the floor (there should be gaps between your back and the floor). Leave your eyes open.

Rest your head on the book without pushing it into the book as you allow your head to release from the top of your spine. Without pulling your chin down, think of your neck as if it were falling away from your head.

When you are ready to stand up, do it slowly and easily. Be aware of your surroundings and leave the exercise until the next time.

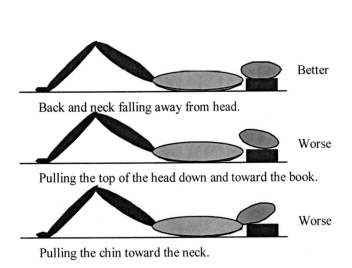

Better
Back and neck falling away from head.

Worse
Pulling the top of the head down and toward the book.

Worse
Pulling the chin toward the neck.

Allow your head to lie level on the book. Avoid pulling the top of your head down toward the book and avoid pulling your chin toward your neck.

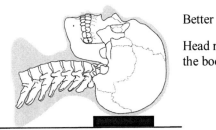

Better
Head resting on the book.

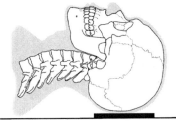

Worse
Head pulled backward and down into the book, shortening the spine.

Your spine reaches all the way to the level of your ears, higher than the roof of your mouth. As you allow your neck to soften, your head will move a little farther from your shoulders, giving your spine room to reach its full length.

Remain open to new discoveries every time you practice the exercise.	Don't rush. Give yourself plenty of time to repeat and understand each instruction.	Look for comfort by waiting for your muscles to soften, not through shifting.

Head/Neck Relationship

6. Your head should rest flat on the book. If your torso is thin and your back is straight when you lie down, use a thin book. If your torso is very thick or bent, use a thicker book or even a stack of books.

The number next to each caption refers to the page where the image originally appeared. For example, the images on this page originally appeared on page 6.

Your head rests at the top of your spine. Your spine meets your head at about the level of your ears, higher than the roof of your mouth. Excess tension in the back of the neck tends to pull the head back and down, toward the neck/spine. This causes crowding between your head and your neck.

With your head on the book, think of allowing your neck to soften, releasing your head from the top of your spine so that your neck will be able to fall a little bit toward the floor. This subtle separation will leave more room between your head and neck, allowing your neck to approach its true length. The book under your head provides some distance between your neck and the floor so that this can happen.

Part I, Section 3. Point Your Spine

Lie on your back with your head on the book, your feet flat on the floor (knees bent) and your hands on your abdomen. Imagine that you are almost weightless. Keep your hands apart and your knees separate from each other. Avoid moving around in order to look for the best position. Without pushing, allow your whole body to settle toward the floor (there should be gaps between your back and the floor). Leave your eyes open.

Rest your head on the book without pushing it into the book as you allow your head to release from the top of your spine. Without pulling your chin down, think of your neck as if it were falling away from your head.

Continuing to release your head from the top of your spine, gently point the top of your spine as if it were reaching past the back of your head.

When you are ready to stand up, do it slowly and easily. Be aware of your surroundings and leave the exercise until the next time.

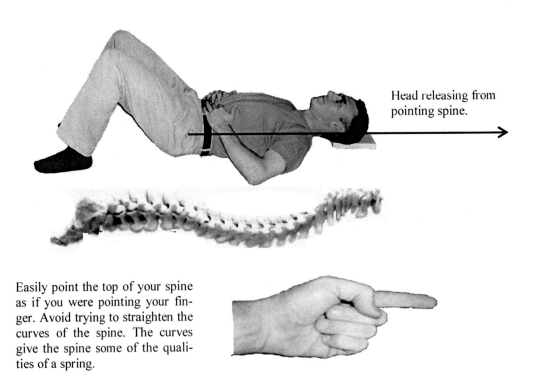

Head releasing from pointing spine.

Easily point the top of your spine as if you were pointing your finger. Avoid trying to straighten the curves of the spine. The curves give the spine some of the qualities of a spring.

Remain open to new discoveries every time you practice the exercise.	Don't rush. Give yourself plenty of time to repeat and understand each instruction.	Look for comfort by waiting for your muscles to soften, not through shifting.

6. Your head should rest flat on the book. If your torso is thin and your back is straight when you lie down, use a thin book. If your torso is very thick or bent, use a thicker book or even a stack of books.

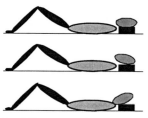

8. Allow your head to lie level on the book. Avoid pulling the top of your head down toward the book and avoid pulling your chin toward your neck.

Better

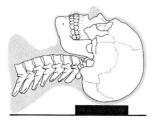

8. Head resting on the book.

Worse

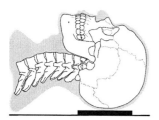

8. Head pulled backward and down into the book, shortening the spine.

Sometimes, Doing a *Little* More

Point with the tip of your index finger. *Don't use more effort than you need,* just point. Keeping your finger pointed, push on something like your other hand or a solid object. Try to use as little force as possible to keep your finger straight. Notice that you can keep your finger straight with very little effort, even if you push fairly hard. As you push, imagine your finger getting longer from the tip down, as if the tip of your finger were reaching to where it is pointing.

Your finger is a column of bones and, in that sense, very much like your spine. In this section, as you allow for a softening in the relationship between your head and spine, you will have room to gently point the top of your spine as if it were reaching past the back of your head.

A Train

Think of your spine as a train with 34 cars, one for each of your vertebrae, with the engine at the top. As you stop pulling your head into your spine, your spine will have some room to lengthen from the top down as it points so that each vertebra gives room for the one below.

Part I, Section 4. Allow Your Ribs to Soften

Lie on your back with your head on the book, your feet flat on the floor (knees bent) and your hands on your abdomen. Imagine that you are almost weightless. Keep your hands apart and your knees separate from each other. Avoid moving around in order to look for the best position. Without pushing, allow your whole body to settle toward the floor (there should be gaps between your back and the floor). Leave your eyes open.

Rest your head on the book without pushing it into the book as you allow your head to release from the top of your spine. Without pulling your chin down, think of your neck as if it were falling away from your head.

Continuing to release your head from the top of your spine, gently point the top of your spine as if it were reaching past the back of your head. **As you continue pointing your spine, allow your ribs to soften as you notice their easy movement in response to your breathing.**

When you are ready to stand up, do it slowly and easily. Be aware of your surroundings and leave the exercise until the next time.

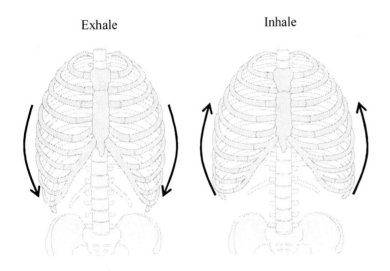

Allow your ribs to swing freely from your pointing spine in response to your breathing. The image demonstrates the maximum amount of movement available. While lying down, your ribs will probably not travel to the extent shown.

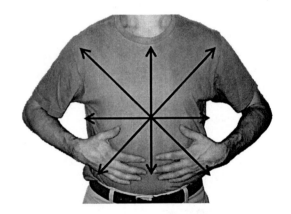

Allow your torso to be open in every direction.

Remain open to new discoveries every time you practice the exercise.	Don't rush. Give yourself plenty of time to repeat and understand each instruction.	Look for comfort by waiting for your muscles to soften, not through shifting.

6. Your head should rest flat on the book. If your torso is thin and your back is straight when you lie down, use a thin book. If your torso is very thick or bent, use a thicker book or even a stack of books.

10. Easily point the top of your spine as if you were pointing your finger. Avoid trying to straighten the curves of the spine. The curves give the spine some of the qualities of a spring.

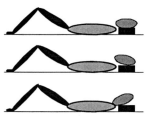

8. Allow your head to lie level on the book. Avoid pulling the top of your head down toward the book and avoid pulling your chin toward your neck.

Better

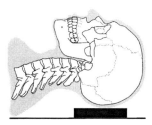

8. Head resting on the book.

Worse

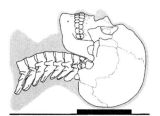

8. Head pulled backward and down into the book, shortening the spine.

The Spine Points, the Ribs Hang

Your ribs, like your head, also attach to your spine. There is a joint for each rib where it attaches to your spine. Your ribs extend from those joints and wrap around you, back to front. It is common for people to internally fix the ribs in place, making breathing and moving more difficult. Allow your ribs to soften so that they can easily move all around you (back, sides, and front).

Openness

You are now about halfway through the first part of the exercise. You may or may not be noticing something different during the exercise. Some people ask, "What am I supposed to be looking for?" It is often described as a feeling of openness or ease. This is not something that you can find by activating your muscles, but only by following the directions: releasing your head from the top of your spine, gently pointing the top of your spine as if it were reaching past the back of your head, and releasing your ribs.

If you are not noticing it, keep waiting and keep looking. Even the slightest difference can be significant.

Part I, Section 5. Point Your Shoulders

Lie on your back with your head on the book, your feet flat on the floor (knees bent) and your hands on your abdomen. Imagine that you are almost weightless. Keep your hands apart and your knees separate from each other. Avoid moving around in order to look for the best position. Without pushing, allow your whole body to settle toward the floor (there should be gaps between your back and the floor). Leave your eyes open.

Rest your head on the book without pushing it into the book as you allow your head to release from the top of your spine. Without pulling your chin down, think of your neck as if it were falling away from your head.

Continuing to release your head from the top of your spine, gently point the top of your spine as if it were reaching past the back of your head. As you continue pointing your spine, allow your ribs to soften as you notice their easy movement in response to your breathing. **Without pushing, allow your shoulders to fall toward the floor as you gently point them away from each other. Allow for widening across your whole torso, front and back, as you continue to allow your ribs to move effortlessly.**

When you are ready to stand up, do it slowly and easily. Be aware of your surroundings and leave the exercise until the next time.

Gently point your shoulders away from each other.

Remain open to new discoveries every time you practice the exercise.	Don't rush. Give yourself plenty of time to repeat and understand each instruction.	Look for comfort by waiting for your muscles to soften, not through shifting.

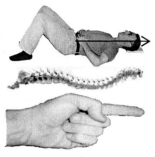

6. Your head should rest flat on the book. If your torso is thin and your back is straight when you lie down, use a thin book. If your torso is very thick or bent, use a thicker book or even a stack of books.

10. Easily point the top of your spine as if you were pointing your finger. Avoid trying to straighten the curves of the spine. The curves give the spine some of the qualities of a spring.

The Shoulders

It is very common for people to pull their shoulders forward and together, causing the chest to narrow and the back to round. The answer is not to pull the shoulders back, but to stop pulling them together and forward. Holding your shoulders back can make your chest wider, but it also makes your back narrower and impinges on arm movement. Sometimes people pull their shoulders up. Again, the answer is not to push them down but to stop pulling them up. There is no need to "hold" your shoulders anywhere.

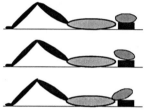

8. Allow your head to lie level on the book. Avoid pulling the top of your head down toward the book and avoid pulling your chin toward your neck.

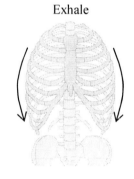

Exhale

Better

8. Head resting on the book.

Worse

Inhale

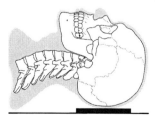

8. Head pulled backward and down into the book, shortening the spine.

12. Allow your ribs to swing freely from your pointing spine in response to your breathing.

Part I, Section 6. Allow Your Wrists to Soften So That Your Arms Can Lengthen

Lie on your back with your head on the book, your feet flat on the floor (knees bent) and your hands on your abdomen. Imagine that you are almost weightless. Keep your hands apart and your knees separate from each other. Avoid moving around in order to look for the best position. Without pushing, allow your whole body to settle toward the floor (there should be gaps between your back and the floor). Leave your eyes open.

Rest your head on the book without pushing it into the book as you allow your head to release from the top of your spine. Without pulling your chin down, think of your neck as if it were falling away from your head.

Continuing to release your head from the top of your spine, gently point the top of your spine as if it were reaching past the back of your head. As you continue pointing your spine, allow your ribs to soften as you notice their easy movement in response to your breathing. Without pushing, allow your shoulders to fall toward the floor as you gently point them away from each other. Allow for widening across your whole torso, front and back, as you continue to allow your ribs to move effortlessly. **Allow your wrists to soften to allow for space between your hands and wrists. Without moving them, think of your arms as lengthening from your hands up to your shoulders.**

When you are ready to stand up, do it slowly and easily. Be aware of your surroundings and leave the exercise until the next time.

Worse   Better

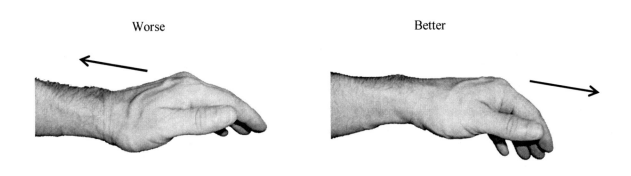

Allow your hands to release from your wrists to allow your arms to lengthen.

Remain open to new discoveries every time you practice the exercise.	Don't rush. Give yourself plenty of time to repeat and understand each instruction.	Look for comfort by waiting for your muscles to soften, not through shifting.

www.freeyourneck.com

The Wrists

Your wrists are like your neck in the way they move, and because your hands are attached to your wrists, your hands are like your head. They are also similar because they are at an extremity of your body. Your head is at the end of your spine and your hands are at the ends of your arms. And just like your head, neck, and spine, if you allow your wrists to soften you might find a little more space between your wrists and your hands, letting you think of your arms as longer.

6. Your head should rest flat on the book. If your torso is thin and your back is straight when you lie down, use a thin book. If your torso is very thick or bent, use a thicker book or even a stack of books.

10. Easily point the top of your spine as if you were pointing your finger. Avoid trying to straighten the curves of the spine. The curves give the spine some of the qualities of a spring.

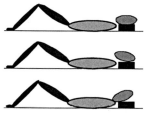

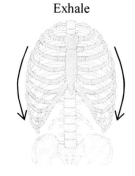

Exhale

8. Allow your head to lie level on the book. Avoid pulling the top of your head down toward the book and avoid pulling your chin toward your neck.

Inhale

Better

8. Head resting on the book.

Worse

8. Head pulled backward and down into the book, shortening the spine.

12. Allow your ribs to swing freely from your pointing spine in response to your breathing.

14. Gently point your shoulders away from each other.

Part I, Section 7. Allow for Space between Your Arms and Torso

Lie on your back with your head on the book, your feet flat on the floor (knees bent) and your hands on your abdomen. Imagine that you are almost weightless. Keep your hands apart and your knees separate from each other. Avoid moving around in order to look for the best position. Without pushing, allow your whole body to settle toward the floor (there should be gaps between your back and the floor). Leave your eyes open.

Rest your head on the book without pushing it into the book as you allow your head to release from the top of your spine. Without pulling your chin down, think of your neck as if it were falling away from your head.

Continuing to release your head from the top of your spine, gently point the top of your spine as if it were reaching past the back of your head. As you continue pointing your spine, allow your ribs to soften as you notice their easy movement in response to your breathing. Without pushing, allow your shoulders to fall toward the floor as you gently point them away from each other. Allow for widening across your whole torso, front and back, as you continue to allow your ribs to move effortlessly. Allow your wrists to soften to allow for space between your hands and wrists. Without moving them, think of your arms as lengthening from your hands up to your shoulders.

Avoid clenching your arms or holding them in a tight position. Without moving your arms, allow the space between your arms and torso to be expansive. Gently point your elbows away from each other just as your shoulders point away from each other and the top of your spine points past the back of your head.

When you are ready to stand up, do it slowly and easily. Be aware of your surroundings and leave the exercise until the next time.

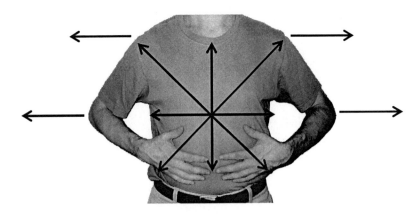

Allow for space between your arms and torso. Point your shoulders and elbows away from each other.

Remain open to new discoveries every time you practice the exercise.	Don't rush. Give yourself plenty of time to repeat and understand each instruction.	Look for comfort by waiting for your muscles to soften, not through shifting.

 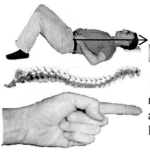 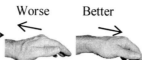

6. Your head should rest flat on the book. If your torso is thin and your back is straight when you lie down, use a thin book. If your torso is very thick or bent, use a thicker book or even a stack of books.

10. Easily point the top of your spine as if you were pointing your finger. Avoid trying to straighten the curves of the spine. The curves give the spine some of the qualities of a spring.

16. Allow your hands to release from your wrists to allow your arms to lengthen.

Avoid Clenching Your Arms
Just like your head, it is generally not useful to hold your arms in a fixed position. Fixing or clenching the arms makes it more difficult to move them. Instead, allow your hands to rest on your abdomen. But don't confuse this with the "right" place for your arms. It is just "a" place for your arms. (For our purposes now it is a good place, but it is not the only place.)

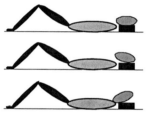

8. Allow your head to lie level on the book. Avoid pulling the top of your head down toward the book and avoid pulling your chin toward your neck.

Exhale

Better

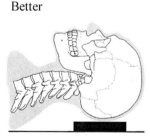

8. Head resting on the book.

Worse

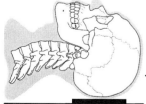

8. Head pulled backward and down into the book, shortening the spine.

Inhale

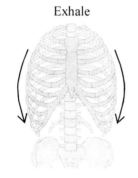

12. Allow your ribs to swing freely from your pointing spine in response to your breathing.

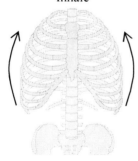

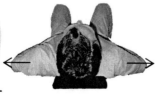

14. Gently point your shoulders away from each other.

Part I, Section 8. Allow Your Hip Sockets to Soften as You Point Your Knees

Lie on your back with your head on the book, your feet flat on the floor (knees bent) and your hands on your abdomen. Imagine that you are almost weightless. Keep your hands apart and your knees separate from each other. Avoid moving around in order to look for the best position. Without pushing, allow your whole body to settle toward the floor (there should be gaps between your back and the floor). Leave your eyes open.

Rest your head on the book without pushing it into the book as you allow your head to release from the top of your spine. Without pulling your chin down, think of your neck as if it were falling away from your head.

Continuing to release your head from the top of your spine, gently point the top of your spine as if it were reaching past the back of your head. As you continue pointing your spine, allow your ribs to soften as you notice their easy movement in response to your breathing. Without pushing, allow your shoulders to fall toward the floor as you gently point them away from each other. Allow for widening across your whole torso, front and back, as you continue to allow your ribs to move effortlessly. Allow your wrists to soften to allow for space between your hands and wrists. Without moving them, think of your arms as lengthening from your hands up to your shoulders.

Avoid clenching your arms or holding them in a tight position. Without moving your arms, allow the space between your arms and torso to be expansive. Gently point your elbows away from each other just as your shoulders point away from each other and the top of your spine points past the back of your head as your head releases from the top of your spine.

Allow your legs to soften in your hip sockets so that your pelvis can fall away from your legs as you gently point your knees toward the ceiling.

When you are ready to stand up, do it slowly and easily. Be aware of your surroundings and leave the exercise until the next time.

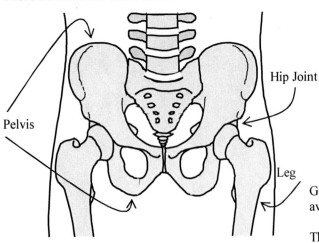

Allow your legs to release from your pelvis.

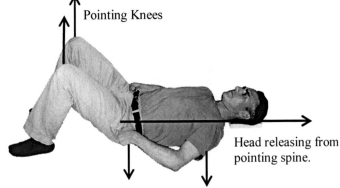

Gently point your knees to the ceiling as you allow your pelvis to fall away from your legs.

The legs attach to the pelvis lower than most people think. To find your hip joints, place your thumbs directly on them (as shown) in the corner where the front of your leg meets your pelvis.

Remain open to new discoveries every time you practice the exercise.	Don't rush. Give yourself plenty of time to repeat and understand each instruction.	Look for comfort by waiting for your muscles to soften, not through shifting.

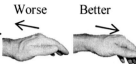

16. Allow your hands to release from your wrists to allow your arms to lengthen.

6. Your head should rest flat on the book. If your torso is thin and your back is straight when you lie down, use a thin book. If your torso is very thick or bent, use a thicker book or even a stack of books.

10. Easily point the top of your spine as if you were pointing your finger. Avoid trying to straighten the curves of the spine. The curves give the spine some of the qualities of a spring.

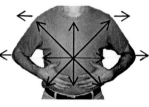

18. Allow for space between your arms and torso. Point your shoulders and elbows away from each other.

Allow Your Legs to Be Free

The lower end of your torso extends all the way to the base of your pelvis. It is at your pelvis that your legs attach to your torso. In the same way that you are allowing your head to be free from the top of your spine and your spine to fall away from your head, you can also allow for your legs to be free from your pelvis and your pelvis to fall away from your legs.

As your pelvis falls away from your legs, expend the minimum effort to point your knees up to the ceiling, just as you are pointing your elbows and your spine. Avoid allowing your legs to fall sideways toward the floor.

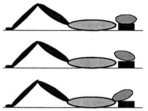

8. Allow your head to lie level on the book. Avoid pulling the top of your head down toward the book and avoid pulling your chin toward your neck.

Exhale

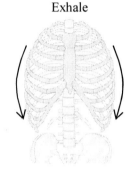

Better

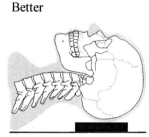

Inhale

8. Head resting on the book.

Worse

12. Allow your ribs to swing freely from your pointing spine in response to your breathing.

8. Head pulled backward and down into the book, shortening the spine.

14. Gently point your shoulders away from each other.

Part I, Section 9. Allow Your Ankles to Soften So That Your Legs Can Lengthen

Lie on your back with your head on the book, your feet flat on the floor (knees bent) and your hands on your abdomen. Imagine that you are almost weightless. Keep your hands apart and your knees separate from each other. Avoid moving around in order to look for the best position. Without pushing, allow your whole body to settle toward the floor (there should be gaps between your back and the floor). Leave your eyes open.

Rest your head on the book without pushing it into the book as you allow your head to release from the top of your spine. Without pulling your chin down, think of your neck as if it were falling away from your head.

Continuing to release your head from the top of your spine, gently point the top of your spine as if it were reaching past the back of your head. As you continue pointing your spine, allow your ribs to soften as you notice their easy movement in response to your breathing. Without pushing, allow your shoulders to fall toward the floor as you gently point them away from each other. Allow for widening across your whole torso, front and back, as you continue to allow your ribs to move effortlessly. Allow your wrists to soften to allow for space between your hands and wrists. Without moving them, think of your arms as lengthening from your hands up to your shoulders.

Avoid clenching your arms or holding them in a tight position. Without moving your arms, allow the space between your arms and torso to be expansive. Gently point your elbows away from each other just as your shoulders point away from each other and the top of your spine points past the back of your head as your head releases from the top of your spine.

Allow your legs to soften in your hip sockets so that your pelvis can fall away from your legs as you gently point your knees toward the ceiling.

Allow your ankle joints to soften to allow for space between your feet and ankle joints. Think of your legs as lengthening from the feet up.

When you are ready to stand up, do it slowly and easily. Be aware of your surroundings and leave the exercise until the next time.

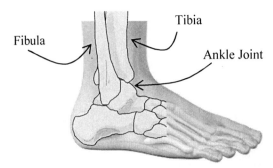

Allow your ankle joints to soften to allow for space between
your feet and ankles and to allow for your legs to lengthen.

Remain open to new discoveries every time you practice the exercise.	Don't rush. Give yourself plenty of time to repeat and understand each instruction.	Look for comfort by waiting for your muscles to soften, not through shifting.

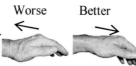

16. Allow your hands to release from your wrists to allow your arms to lengthen.

Ankles, Feet, and Legs

Just like your wrists and your neck, as you allow your ankles to soften, your feet will be able to come away a little from your ankles, giving your legs a little bit of room to lengthen.

The ankles, wrists, and neck are similar joints in that they are all at the extremity of your body and there is a lot of mobility. But also, anything that you discover about one, in terms of ease and space, is true for them all.

6. Your head should rest flat on the book. If your torso is thin and your back is straight when you lie down, use a thin book. If your torso is very thick or bent, use a thicker book or even a stack of books.

10. Easily point the top of your spine as if you were pointing your finger. Avoid trying to straighten the curves of the spine. The curves give the spine some of the qualities of a spring.

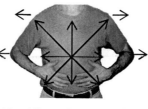

18. Allow for space between your arms and torso. Point your shoulders and elbows away from each other.

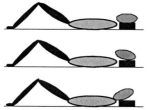

8. Allow your head to lie level on the book. Avoid pulling the top of your head down toward the book and avoid pulling your chin toward your neck.

Exhale

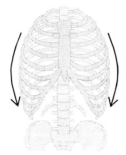

20. Gently point your knees to the ceiling as you allow your pelvis to fall away from your legs.

Better

8. Head resting on the book.

Worse

Inhale

12. Allow your ribs to swing freely from your pointing spine in response to your breathing.

8. Head pulled backward and down into the book, shortening the spine.

14. Gently point your shoulders away from each other.

Part I, Section 10. Allow for Space behind Your Legs

Lie on your back with your head on the book, your feet flat on the floor (knees bent) and your hands on your abdomen. Imagine that you are almost weightless. Keep your hands apart and your knees separate from each other. Avoid moving around in order to look for the best position. Without pushing, allow your whole body to settle toward the floor (there should be gaps between your back and the floor). Leave your eyes open.

Rest your head on the book without pushing it into the book as you allow your head to release from the top of your spine. Without pulling your chin down, think of your neck as if it were falling away from your head.

Continuing to release your head from the top of your spine, gently point the top of your spine as if it were reaching past the back of your head. As you continue pointing your spine, allow your ribs to soften as you notice their easy movement in response to your breathing. Without pushing, allow your shoulders to fall toward the floor as you gently point them away from each other. Allow for widening across your whole torso, front and back, as you continue to allow your ribs to move effortlessly. Allow your wrists to soften to allow for space between your hands and wrists. Without moving them, think of your arms as lengthening from your hands up to your shoulders.

Avoid clenching your arms or holding them in a tight position. Without moving your arms, allow the space between your arms and torso to be expansive. Gently point your elbows away from each other just as your shoulders point away from each other and the top of your spine points past the back of your head as your head releases from the top of your spine.

Allow your legs to soften in your hip sockets so that your pelvis can fall away from your legs as you gently point your knees toward the ceiling.

Allow your ankle joints to soften to allow for space between your feet and ankle joints. Think of your legs as lengthening from the feet up. **Without moving your legs, allow for space behind your legs. Avoid clenching your feet or preventing them from sliding away.**

When you are ready to stand up, do it slowly and easily. Be aware of your surroundings and leave the exercise until the next time.

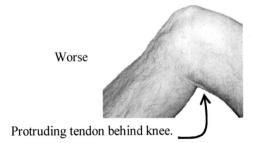   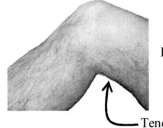

Worse — Protruding tendon behind knee.   Better — Tendon no longer protruding.

As you allow for space behind your leg, the protruding tendon should soften.

Remain open to new discoveries every time you practice the exercise.	Don't rush. Give yourself plenty of time to repeat and understand each instruction.	Look for comfort by waiting for your muscles to soften, not through shifting.

www.freeyourneck.com

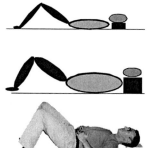

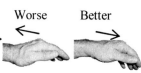

Worse   Better

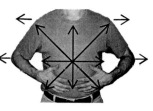

16. Allow your hands to release from your wrists to allow your arms to lengthen.

6. Your head should rest flat on the book. If your torso is thin and your back is straight when you lie down, use a thin book. If your torso is very thick or bent, use a thicker book or even a stack of books.

10. Easily point the top of your spine as if you were pointing your finger. Avoid trying to straighten the curves of the spine. The curves give the spine some of the qualities of a spring.

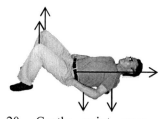

18. Allow for space between your arms and torso. Point your shoulders and elbows away from each other.

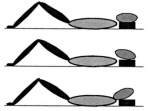

8. Allow your head to lie level on the book. Avoid pulling the top of your head down toward the book and avoid pulling your chin toward your neck.

Better

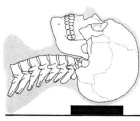

8. Head resting on the book.

Worse

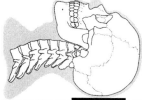

8. Head pulled backward and down into the book, shortening the spine.

Exhale

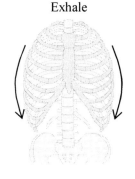

Inhale

12. Allow your ribs to swing freely from your pointing spine in response to your breathing.

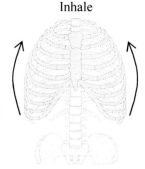

14. Gently point your shoulders away from each other.

20. Gently point your knees to the ceiling as you allow your pelvis to fall away from your legs.

Fibula   Tibia

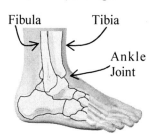

Ankle Joint

22. Allow your ankle joints to soften to allow for space between your feet and ankles and to allow for your legs to lengthen.

Space behind Your Legs

The space behind your legs is very similar to the space between your arms and your torso. As you continue to avoid clenching your legs or pulling your feet toward you, your legs will feel longer.

Sliding Feet

Do not work to prevent your feet from sliding along the floor. There should be enough friction between your feet and the floor to prevent them from sliding.

Part I, Section 11. Lying Down in Full

Lie on your back with your head on the book, your feet flat on the floor (knees bent) and your hands on your abdomen. Imagine that you are almost weightless. Keep your hands apart and your knees separate from each other. Avoid moving around in order to look for the best position. Without pushing, allow your whole body to settle toward the floor (there should be gaps between your back and the floor). Leave your eyes open.

Rest your head on the book without pushing it into the book as you allow your head to release from the top of your spine. Without pulling your chin down, think of your neck as if it were falling away from your head.

Continuing to release your head from the top of your spine, gently point the top of your spine as if it were reaching past the back of your head. As you continue pointing your spine, allow your ribs to soften as you notice their easy movement in response to your breathing. Without pushing, allow your shoulders to fall toward the floor as you gently point them away from each other. Allow for widening across your whole torso, front and back, as you continue to allow your ribs to move effortlessly. Allow your wrists to soften to allow for space between your hands and wrists. Without moving them, think of your arms as lengthening from your hands up to your shoulders.

Avoid clenching your arms or holding them in a tight position. Without moving your arms, allow the space between your arms and torso to be expansive. Gently point your elbows away from each other just as your shoulders point away from each other and the top of your spine points past the back of your head as your head releases from the top of your spine.

Allow your legs to soften in your hip sockets so that your pelvis can fall away from your legs as you gently point your knees toward the ceiling.

Allow your ankle joints to soften to allow for space between your feet and ankle joints. Think of your legs as lengthening from the feet up. Without moving your legs, allow for space behind your legs. Avoid clenching your feet or preventing them from sliding away.

When you are ready to stand up, do it slowly and easily. Be aware of your surroundings and leave the exercise until the next time.

Remain open to new discoveries every time you practice the exercise.	Don't rush. Give yourself plenty of time to repeat and understand each instruction.	Look for comfort by waiting for your muscles to soften, not through shifting.

www.freeyourneck.com

6. Your head should rest flat on the book. If your torso is thin and your back is straight when you lie down, use a thin book. If your torso is very thick or bent, use a thicker book or even a stack of books.

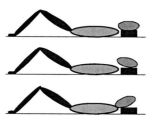

8. Allow your head to lie level on the book. Avoid pulling the top of your head down toward the book and avoid pulling your chin toward your neck.

Better

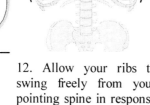

8. Head resting on the book.

Worse

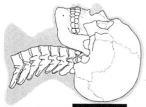

8. Head pulled backward and down into the book, shortening the spine.

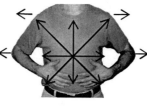

10. Easily point the top of your spine as if you were pointing your finger. Avoid trying to straighten the curves of the spine. The curves give the spine some of the qualities of a spring.

Exhale

Inhale

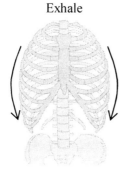

12. Allow your ribs to swing freely from your pointing spine in response to your breathing.

14. Gently point your shoulders away from each other.

Worse   Better

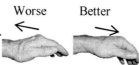

16. Allow your hands to release from your wrists to allow your arms to lengthen.

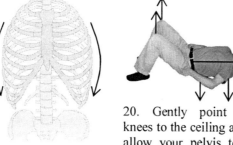

18. Allow for space between your arms and torso. Point your shoulders and elbows away from each other.

20. Gently point your knees to the ceiling as you allow your pelvis to fall away from your legs.

Fibula   Tibia

Ankle Joint

22. Allow your ankle joints to soften to allow for space between your feet and ankles and to allow for your legs to lengthen.

Worse   Better

24. As you allow for space behind your leg, the protruding tendon should soften.

Part I Summary

You have now learned Part I. I hope that you are finding a little extra space (and added comfort) within your body while you are engaged in the exercise. The next step is to find that space, and more, as you begin to move while lying down.

You will find that the lying down portion is the basis for the rest of the exercise and you will recognize it in every new part and section. As you add new sections, always start with lying down and always approach the exercise with an expectation of discovering something new.

As you continue working on Part I, even as you progress through the other parts of the exercise, look for the similarities in the different lying down sections. For example:

- All the joints soften.
- The arms and legs lengthen from the extremity inward.
- The spine, shoulders, elbows, and knees point.

You can think of them all separately, but you can also begin to combine the various sections in your mind so that Part I becomes almost like one thought. In this way you might find that as you learn it, you can complete Part I both quickly and effectively.

If you want, you can use the lying down part of the exercise on its own, even as you progress through the rest of the book. You can set up in a formal way with a book under your head, or you can do it informally as time and interest allow. You can do it in bed as you fall asleep or wake up, or really anywhere you find yourself waiting with nothing to do. You don't have to adjust your position or do anything to prepare. Just start as you are.

Part II

Finding Room As You Move

Before You Begin

In Part I, every section of the exercise is geared toward helping you establish a new *condition* for the normal state of your body. In this new condition, this new state of normal, you are allowing for extra room within your body as you allow your head and ribs to release from your pointing spine, and your arms and legs to release from your torso.

In the second part of the exercise you will allow for the same extra room (the same new condition) that you have found while lying down as you also add moving your legs and arms. Just as people tend to shorten and narrow their body when lying still, they tend to do this even more as they move. This tendency is part of the fabric of our lives and when our energy level goes up, the tendency to shorten and narrow the body goes up with it. Leaving your body more open as you move can make every movement easier, more graceful, and stronger. Although you will practice this part of the exercise while lying down, the skills you develop here are directly applicable to later parts of the exercise where you will stand.

The end of Part I will leave you ready to begin the four sections of Part II seamlessly as you lie on the floor. The activity is to **continue discovering the conditions that you have been establishing in Part I**, while you lift one leg and arm at a time as if you were walking. Your objective is to avoid compromising the release of your head from the top of your spine, your softening ribs, etc. (all the work you have been doing so far) for the sake of the movement. **The movement is always secondary to allowing for room within your body.**

Every time, before you practice Part II, practice Part I first. Then spend 1–5 minutes on Part II of the exercise, more if you like. Remember that as you add Part II, you do not need to lengthen the amount of time you spend on the whole exercise.

As you practice the exercise, you may discover a subtle difference in how you experience your body. Try to remain open to new discoveries every time. When you are ready to stand up, do it slowly and easily. Be aware of your surroundings and leave the exercise until the next time you practice it.

Equipment

The equipment is the same as in Part I. You will need a mat or rug to lie on (something comfortable but firm) and a soft-cover book on which to place your head. You can put a towel over the book if you want. A pillow is too soft. If your torso is very thick or bent, you can use a stack of books. Your feet can be bare or you can wear shoes as long as your feet are not able to slide on the floor.

www.freeyourneck.com

www.freeyourneck.com

Part II, Section 1. Lift Your Arms and Legs

After practicing Part I, continue throughout to discover the conditions previously established (for example, continue to allow your head to release from the top of your pointing spine as you also allow your ribs to soften, etc.) **while, as effortlessly as possible, you lift one leg at a time as if you were walking. Avoid letting your leg fall heavily each time you place your foot back on the floor.**

To add the movement of your arms, continue to allow your head to release from the top of your pointing spine as you also allow your ribs to soften. **At the same time, as effortlessly as possible, lift the arm opposite your rising leg to approximate your arms swinging as if you were walking. Avoid letting your arm drop each time you place it back on the floor. Continue this activity for 30–60 seconds.**

When you are ready to stand up, do it slowly and easily. Be aware of your surroundings and leave the exercise until the next time.

Your spine reaches all the way to the level of your ears, higher than the roof of your mouth. As you allow your neck to soften, your head will move a little farther from your shoulders, giving your spine room to reach its full length.

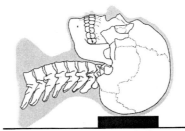

Better

Head resting on the book.

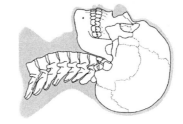

Worse

Head pulled backward and down into the book, shortening the spine.

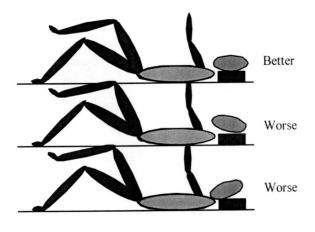

Better

Worse

Worse

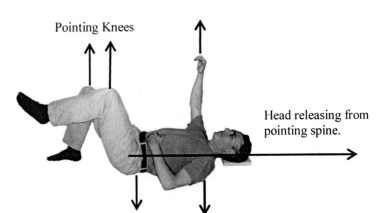

Pointing Knees

Head releasing from pointing spine.

Let your torso and head stay the same as they were as you lift your leg and arm.

Remain open to new discoveries every time you practice the exercise.	Don't rush. Give yourself plenty of time to repeat and understand each instruction.	Look for comfort by waiting for your muscles to soften, not through shifting.

How Can You Do Something without Effort?

All movement requires effort, but people tend to put too much or misplaced effort into movement.

During this part of the exercise, you are lifting one arm and leg as if you were walking. As you do this simple movement, practice trying to leave your head, neck, and torso as they were before you started lifting your arms and legs. You will have to use some effort to move, but you can also experiment to see how little effort it takes. The increased space you have allowed for actually serves to reduce the effort required for movement. You may be surprised to see how easily you can make your leg rise. Especially avoid pushing your head backwards into the book. Allow your head to just rest on the book as you lift your arm and leg.

Part II, Section 2. Clarify Your Hip Joints

After practicing Part I, continue throughout to discover the conditions previously established (for example, continue to allow your head to release from the top of your pointing spine as you also allow your ribs to soften, etc.) while, as effortlessly as possible, you lift one leg at a time as if you were walking. Avoid letting your leg fall heavily each time you place your foot back on the floor.

To add the movement of your arms, continue to allow your head to release from the top of your pointing spine as you also allow your ribs to soften. At the same time, as effortlessly as possible, lift the arm opposite your rising leg to approximate your arms swinging as if you were walking. Avoid letting your arm drop each time you place it back on the floor. Continue this activity for 30–60 seconds.

Stop moving your arms and place your thumbs at the joints where your legs meet your torso. Notice that your legs are moving while your torso stays relatively motionless, almost as it was before you started moving your legs. Continue this activity for 15–30 seconds.

When you are ready to stand up, do it slowly and easily. Be aware of your surroundings and leave the exercise until the next time.

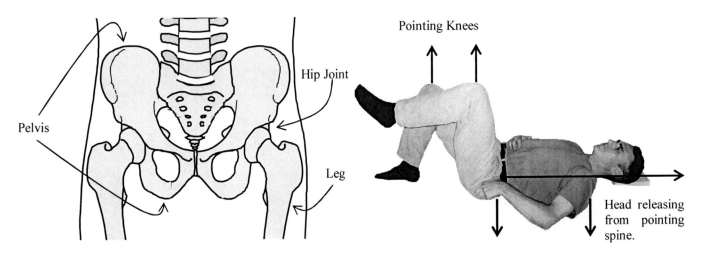

Allow your hips to remain still as your legs move. Place your thumbs in your hip joints as shown to better understand where they are.

Remain open to new discoveries every time you practice the exercise.	Don't rush. Give yourself plenty of time to repeat and understand each instruction.	Look for comfort by waiting for your muscles to soften, not through shifting.

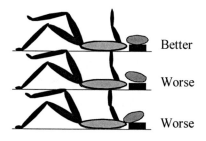

Better

Worse

Worse

Pointing Knees

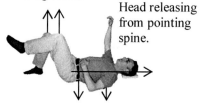

Head releasing from pointing spine.

30. Let your torso and head stay the same as they were as you lift your leg and arm.

Better

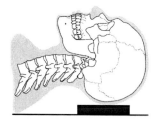

30. Head resting on the book.

Worse

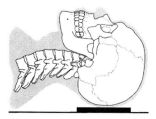

30. Head pulled backward and down into the book, shortening the spine.

30. Your spine reaches all the way to the level of your ears, higher than the roof of your mouth. As you allow your neck to soften, your head will move a little farther from your shoulders, giving your spine room to reach its full length.

Where Do Your Legs Attach to Your Torso?

Your legs connect to your torso at the hip joints. Discovering and properly using your hip joints is a big step in improving both the ease and effectiveness of how you move. The hip joints are probably lower on your body than where you think they are. Use this opportunity to clarify where your legs meet your torso.

During this section you are lifting one leg at a time while continuing to allow for the conditions from Part I. Be sure to notice how you can allow your torso to remain relatively motionless and on the ground, as it was before you were moving your legs. Notice how you can continue to allow your head to release from the top of your pointing spine as you also allow your ribs to soften.

Part II, Section 3. Clarify Your Shoulder Joints

After practicing Part I, continue throughout to discover the conditions previously established (for example, continue to allow your head to release from the top of your pointing spine as you also allow your ribs to soften, etc.) while, as effortlessly as possible, you lift one leg at a time as if you were walking. Avoid letting your leg fall heavily each time you place your foot back on the floor.

To add the movement of your arms, continue to allow your head to release from the top of your pointing spine as you also allow your ribs to soften. At the same time, as effortlessly as possible, lift the arm opposite your rising leg to approximate your arms swinging as if you were walking. Avoid letting your arm drop each time you place it back on the floor. Continue this activity for 30–60 seconds.

Stop moving your arms and place your thumbs at the joints where your legs meet your torso. Notice that your legs are moving while your torso stays relatively motionless, almost as it was before you started moving your legs. Continue this activity for 15–30 seconds.

Let your feet rest on the floor and start swinging your arms again as you did previously. Without pushing or effort, allow your shoulders to rest on the ground as much as possible. Recognize that what rises is your arm and what stays on the floor is your shoulder. With your mind's eye, look for where your shoulders end and your arms begin. Continue this activity for 15–30 seconds.

When you are ready to stand up, do it slowly and easily. Be aware of your surroundings and leave the exercise until the next time.

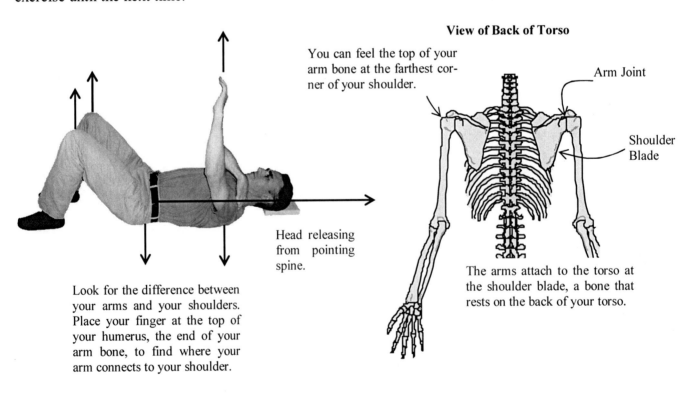

View of Back of Torso

You can feel the top of your arm bone at the farthest corner of your shoulder.

Arm Joint

Shoulder Blade

Head releasing from pointing spine.

Look for the difference between your arms and your shoulders. Place your finger at the top of your humerus, the end of your arm bone, to find where your arm connects to your shoulder.

The arms attach to the torso at the shoulder blade, a bone that rests on the back of your torso.

Remain open to new discoveries every time you practice the exercise.	Don't rush. Give yourself plenty of time to repeat and understand each instruction.	Look for comfort by waiting for your muscles to soften, not through shifting.

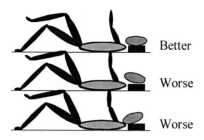

Better

Worse

Worse

Pointing Knees

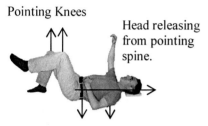

Head releasing from pointing spine.

30. Let your torso and head stay the same as they were as you lift your leg and arm.

Better

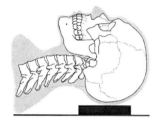

30. Head resting on the book.

Worse

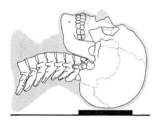

30. Head pulled backward and down into the book, shortening the spine.

30. Your spine reaches all the way to the level of your ears, higher than the roof of your mouth. As you allow your neck to soften, your head will move a little farther from your shoulders, giving your spine room to reach its full length.

Pointing Knees

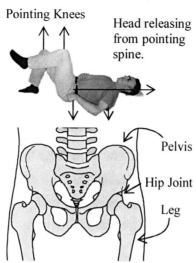

Head releasing from pointing spine.

Pelvis

Hip Joint

Leg

32. Allow your hips to remain still as your legs move. Place your thumbs in your hip joints as shown to better understand where they are.

Where Do Your Arms Attach to Your Torso?

People generally think of their arms as attaching to the front of the torso, but actually they attach more to the back of the torso. Most of the strength in your arms also comes from the musculature in the back of your torso. Your arms attach mostly to, and move from, a large shoulder bone called the scapula or shoulder blade. The scapula is located mostly in the back of your torso.

Your shoulders are part of your torso and they are the structure from which your arms project. Often, people unnecessarily use their shoulders as part of their arms, reaching the shoulders forward with the arms instead of leaving the shoulders back with the rest of the torso. This compromises the strength of the shoulders and the arms. It also constricts the chest, making movement of the arms and the torso more difficult.

As you practice this section, notice width across the front and back of your torso as well as ease in your neck as your arms move. As you lift each arm, try to leave your shoulders as they are. Think of your arms moving off the back of your torso, not the front of your torso.

Part II, Section 4. Part II in Full

After practicing Part I, continue throughout to discover the conditions previously established (for example, continue to allow your head to release from the top of your pointing spine as you also allow your ribs to soften, etc.) while, as effortlessly as possible, you lift one leg at a time as if you were walking. Avoid letting your leg fall heavily each time you place your foot back on the floor.

To add the movement of your arms, continue to allow your head to release from the top of your pointing spine as you also allow your ribs to soften. At the same time, as effortlessly as possible, lift the arm opposite your rising leg to approximate your arms swinging as if you were walking. Avoid letting your arm drop each time you place it back on the floor. Continue this activity for 30–60 seconds.

Stop moving your arms and place your thumbs at the joints where your legs meet your torso. Notice that your legs are moving while your torso stays relatively motionless, almost as it was before you started moving your legs. Continue this activity for 15–30 seconds.

Let your feet rest on the floor and start swinging your arms again as you did previously. Without pushing or effort, allow your shoulders to rest on the ground as much as possible. Recognize that what rises is your arm and what stays on the floor is your shoulder. With your mind's eye, look for where your shoulders end and your arms begin. Continue this activity for 15–30 seconds.

When you are ready to stand up, do it slowly and easily. Be aware of your surroundings and leave the exercise until the next time.

Remain open to new discoveries every time you practice the exercise.	Don't rush. Give yourself plenty of time to repeat and understand each instruction.	Look for comfort by waiting for your muscles to soften, not through shifting.

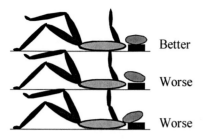

Better

Worse

Worse

Pointing Knees

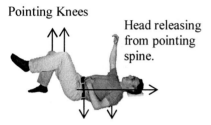

Head releasing from pointing spine.

30. Let your torso and head stay the same as they were as you lift your leg and arm.

Better

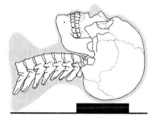

30. Head resting on the book.

Worse

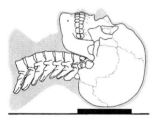

30. Head pulled backward and down into the book, shortening the spine.

30. Your spine reaches all the way to the level of your ears, higher than the roof of your mouth. As you allow your neck to soften, your head will move a little farther from your shoulders, giving your spine room to reach its full length.

Pointing Knees

Head releasing from pointing spine.

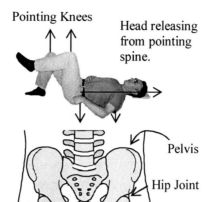

Pelvis

Hip Joint

Leg

32. Allow your hips to remain still as your legs move. Place your thumbs in your hip joints as shown to better understand where they are.

Pointing Knees

Head releasing from pointing spine.

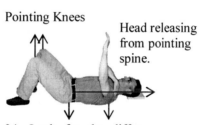

34. Look for the difference between your arms and your shoulders. Place your finger at the top of your humerus, the end of your arm bone, to find where your arm connects to your shoulder. You can feel the top of your arm bone at the farthest corner of your shoulder.

34. Back of Torso

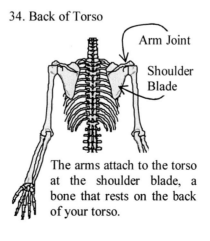

Arm Joint

Shoulder Blade

The arms attach to the torso at the shoulder blade, a bone that rests on the back of your torso.

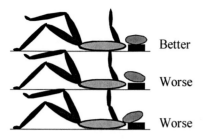

Part II Summary

You have now discovered and practiced the skill of allowing for length and width within your body while lying still and while adding the movement of your arms and legs. You have also begun to clarify where your torso ends and your arms and legs begin. Although you are still lying down, these skills are all key building blocks for standing and moving with more ease and grace and you will continue to use them as the exercise progresses.

Part III

Semi-Vertical

Before You Begin

In this third part of the exercise you will again explore the idea that there is more room available to you than you realize. The difference is that you will be in a semi-vertical position leaning against a wall. If people shorten and narrow their bodies when simply lying down, they certainly do it even more when standing. This is a major factor in poor posture and movement but you can learn to apply the skills you are developing in the lying down portion of the exercise toward permanently standing at your full height. The challenge of allowing for a more open body is greater while standing than when lying down but the benefits include looking taller and feeling more comfortable. Your pointing spine will still point, but now it will point up.

After finishing Part II, gently get up and lean against a wall as shown below to begin the ten sections of Part III. Keep your feet about shoulder-width apart and about 14 inches away from the wall. **Do not push any part of your back against the wall, just lean**. Leave your arms at your sides. Make sure that your pelvis is resting against the wall and that your head is not against the wall. The activity for Part III, virtually the same as Part I except in a semi-vertical position, is to lean against a wall **while discovering the conditions for everything that you just went through in Parts I and II.**

Every time, before you practice Part III, practice Parts I and II first. Then spend 1–5 minutes (or more) on Part III each time you do it. Remember, as you add the ten sections of Part III, you do not need to lengthen the time you spend doing the whole exercise.

As you practice the exercise, you may discover a subtle difference in how you experience your body. Try to remain open to new discoveries every time. When you walk away from the wall, do it slowly and easily. Be aware of your surroundings and leave the exercise until the next time you practice it.

Equipment

A smooth wall with no obstructions from the floor to your full height and width, and clothing that can slide easily along the wall. Your feet can be bare or you can wear shoes as long as your feet are not able to slide on the floor.

       ©2010 Leland Vall

Part III, Section 1. Allow Yourself to Lean against the Wall

After practicing Parts I and II, **gently stand up and lean your torso against a wall, including your pelvis but not your head. Imagine that leaning is as easy as lying down. Avoid moving around in order to look for the best position. Without pushing, allow your back to rest against the wall (there will be some gaps between your back and the wall). Leave your eyes open.**

When you are ready to end the exercise, bring your feet together and step backwards until your heels touch the wall. As you take your first step away from the wall, let your pelvis be the last part of you touching the wall. Be aware of your surroundings and leave the exercise until the next time.

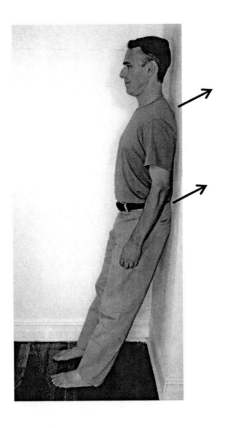

Allow your back to settle against the wall. Since there is no book, your head will not touch anything. Do not pull your head back or forward.

Better   Worse

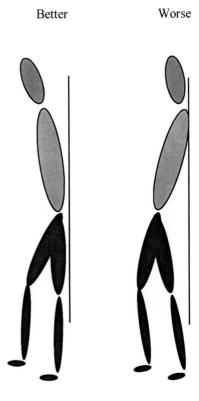

Walking away from the wall, let your pelvis be the last part of you touching the wall.

Remain open to new discoveries every time you practice the exercise.	Don't rush. Give yourself plenty of time to repeat and understand each instruction.	Look for comfort by waiting for your muscles to soften, not through shifting.

Leaning as Lying

Leaning against the wall turns the lying down portion onto its feet. Just as when you are lying down, your back is still resting against something here but now it is the wall. It may not be easy at first, but try to imagine that this position is as easy as lying down. The wall is, at least partially, holding you up.

Part III, Section 2. Allow Your Head to Release from the Top of Your Spine

After practicing Parts I and II, gently stand up and lean your torso against a wall, including your pelvis but not your head. Imagine that leaning is as easy as lying down. Avoid moving around in order to look for the best position. Without pushing, allow your back to rest against the wall (there will be some gaps between your back and the wall). Leave your eyes open. **With your mind's eye, look for the top of your spine, somewhere about the level of your ears and higher than the roof of your mouth. As your torso settles back, gently allow your head to become free from the top of your spine, as if it were resting on the book.**

When you are ready to end the exercise, bring your feet together and step backwards until your heels touch the wall. As you take your first step away from the wall, let your pelvis be the last part of you touching the wall. Be aware of your surroundings and leave the exercise until the next time.

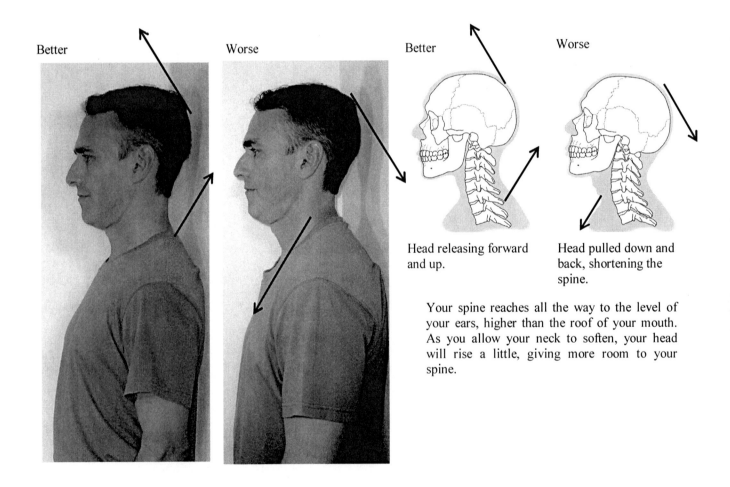

Better   Worse   Better   Worse

Head releasing forward and up.

Head pulled down and back, shortening the spine.

Your spine reaches all the way to the level of your ears, higher than the roof of your mouth. As you allow your neck to soften, your head will rise a little, giving more room to your spine.

Remain open to new discoveries every time you practice the exercise.	Don't rush. Give yourself plenty of time to repeat and understand each instruction.	Look for comfort by waiting for your muscles to soften, not through shifting.

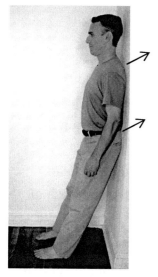

40. Allow your back to settle against the wall. Since there is no book, your head will not touch anything. Do not pull your head back or forward.

Better   Worse

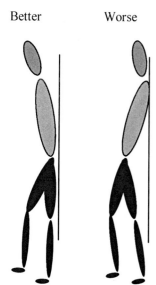

40. Walking away from the wall, let your pelvis be the last part of you touching the wall.

Head/Neck Relationship

Your head sits at the top of your spine. Your spine meets your head at about the level of your ears, higher than the roof of your mouth. Whether you feel it or not, it is very common for people to pull the head back and down, toward the neck/spine. This causes crowding between your head and your neck.

As you lean against the wall, without pushing or forcing, allow your whole torso and neck to settle toward the wall. **Your neck will not actually touch the wall, but you can allow your neck to drift toward the wall.** As your neck and torso settle toward the wall, allow your head to remain where it is, as if your neck were moving away from your head.

Just as when you had your head on the book, this leaving your head forward as your neck and torso drift back will allow your head to rotate slightly forward and up, giving your spine more room. As you allow for this release of your head you are learning to hold your head with less effort.

Part III, Section 3. Point Your Spine

After practicing Parts I and II, gently stand up and lean your torso against a wall, including your pelvis but not your head. Imagine that leaning is as easy as lying down. Avoid moving around in order to look for the best position. Without pushing, allow your back to rest against the wall (there will be some gaps between your back and the wall). Leave your eyes open. With your mind's eye, look for the top of your spine, somewhere about the level of your ears and higher than the roof of your mouth. As your back falls back, gently leave your head where it is, as if it were resting on the book. **Continuing to release your head from the top of your spine, gently point the top of your spine as if it were reaching past the back of your head.**

When you are ready to end the exercise, bring your feet together and step backwards until your heels touch the wall. As you take your first step away from the wall, let your pelvis be the last part of you touching the wall. Be aware of your surroundings and leave the exercise until the next time.

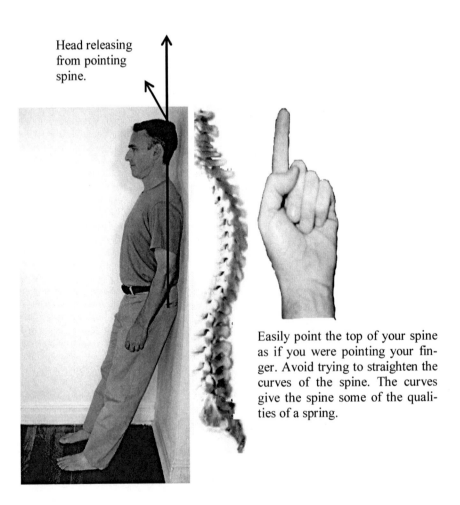

Head releasing from pointing spine.

Easily point the top of your spine as if you were pointing your finger. Avoid trying to straighten the curves of the spine. The curves give the spine some of the qualities of a spring.

Remain open to new discoveries every time you practice the exercise.	Don't rush. Give yourself plenty of time to repeat and understand each instruction.	Look for comfort by waiting for your muscles to soften, not through shifting.

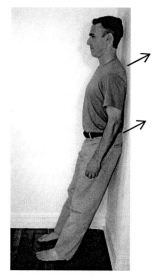

40. Allow your back to settle against the wall. Since there is no book, your head will not touch anything. Do not pull your head back or forward.

Better   Worse

40. Walking away from the wall, let your pelvis be the last part of you touching the wall.

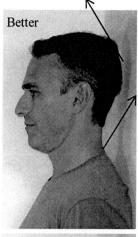

Better

Worse

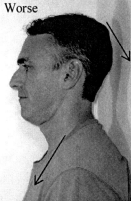

Better

42. Head releasing forward and up.

Worse

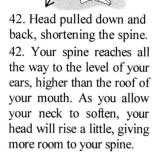

42. Head pulled down and back, shortening the spine.

42. Your spine reaches all the way to the level of your ears, higher than the roof of your mouth. As you allow your neck to soften, your head will rise a little, giving more room to your spine.

Sometimes, Doing a *Little* More

Point with the tip of your index finger. *Don't use more effort than you need,* just point. Keeping your finger pointed, push on something like your other hand or a solid object. Try to use as little force as possible to keep your finger straight. Notice that you can keep your finger straight with very little effort, even if you push fairly hard. As you push, imagine your finger getting longer from the tip down, as if the tip of your finger were reaching to where it is pointing.

Your finger is a column of bones and, in that sense, very much like your spine. In this section, as you allow for a softening in the relationship between your head and spine, you will have room to gently point the top of your spine as if it were reaching past the back of your head.

A Train

Think of your spine as a train with 34 cars, one for each of your vertebrae with the engine at the top. As your head rises it will leave some room for your spine to lengthen from the top down as the engine pulls away, letting each vertebra rise a little bit from the one below.

Part III, Section 4. Allow Your Ribs to Soften

After practicing Parts I and II, gently stand up and lean your torso against a wall, including your pelvis but not your head. Imagine that leaning is as easy as lying down. Avoid moving around in order to look for the best position. Without pushing, allow your back to rest against the wall (there will be some gaps between your back and the wall). Leave your eyes open. With your mind's eye, look for the top of your spine, somewhere about the level of your ears and higher than the roof of your mouth. As your torso settles back, gently allow your head to become free from the top of your spine, as if it were resting on the book. Continuing to release your head from the top of your spine, gently point the top of your spine as if it were reaching past the back of your head.

Allow your ribs to hang softly from your pointing spine as you notice their effortless movement (front, sides, and back) in response to your breathing.

When you are ready to end the exercise, bring your feet together and step backwards until your heels touch the wall. As you take your first step away from the wall, let your pelvis be the last part of you touching the wall. Be aware of your surroundings and leave the exercise until the next time.

Exhale   Inhale

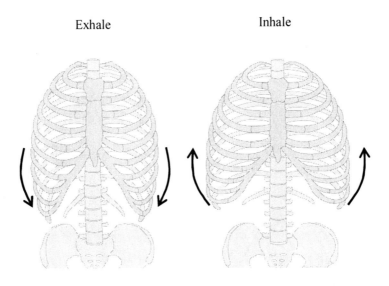

Allow your ribs to swing freely from your pointing spine.

Remain open to new discoveries every time you practice the exercise.	Don't rush. Give yourself plenty of time to repeat and understand each instruction.	Look for comfort by waiting for your muscles to soften, not through shifting.

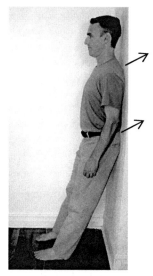

40. Allow your back to settle against the wall. Since there is no book, your head will not touch anything. Do not pull your head back or forward.

Better   Worse

40. Walking away from the wall, let your pelvis be the last part of you touching the wall.

Better

Worse

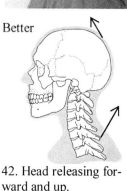

Better

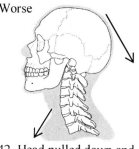

42. Head releasing forward and up.

Worse

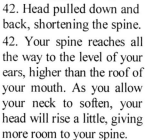

42. Head pulled down and back, shortening the spine.
42. Your spine reaches all the way to the level of your ears, higher than the roof of your mouth. As you allow your neck to soften, your head will rise a little, giving more room to your spine.

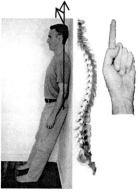

Head releasing from pointing spine.

44. Easily point the top of your spine as if you were pointing your finger. Avoid trying to straighten the curves of the spine. The curves give the spine some of the qualities of a spring.

The Spine Points, the Ribs Hang

Your ribs, like your head, also attach to your spine. There is a joint for each rib where it attaches to your spine. Your ribs extend from those joints and wrap around you back to front. It is common for people to internally fix the ribs in place, making breathing and moving more difficult. People often use their ribs to hold up the torso, a job that is better reserved for the pointing spine.

Instead of holding your ribs, allow them to soften so that they can hang from your pointing spine, easily moving all around you (back, sides, and front) as your ribs respond to breath.

The Swinging Ribs

The ribs have attachments both in the back and front. In the back they attach to your spine and in the front they come together at your sternum. If your ribs are moving freely, they swing on these two points like bucket handles.

Part III, Section 5. Point Your Shoulders

After practicing Parts I and II, gently stand up and lean your torso against a wall, including your pelvis but not your head. Imagine that leaning is as easy as lying down. Avoid moving around in order to look for the best position. Without pushing, allow your back to rest against the wall (there will be some gaps between your back and the wall). Leave your eyes open. With your mind's eye, look for the top of your spine, somewhere about the level of your ears and higher than the roof of your mouth. As your torso settles back, gently allow your head to become free from the top of your spine, as if it were resting on the book. Continuing to release your head from the top of your spine, gently point the top of your spine as if it were reaching past the back of your head.

Allow your ribs to hang softly from your pointing spine as you notice their effortless movement (front, sides, and back) in response to your breathing. **Without pushing, allow your shoulders to drift toward the wall as you gently point them away from each other. Allow for widening across your whole torso, front and back, as you continue to allow your hanging ribs to move effortlessly on your pointing spine.**

When you are ready to end the exercise, bring your feet together and step backwards until your heels touch the wall. As you take your first step away from the wall, let your pelvis be the last part of you touching the wall. Be aware of your surroundings and leave the exercise until the next time.

Gently point your shoulders away from each other.

Remain open to new discoveries every time you practice the exercise.	Don't rush. Give yourself plenty of time to repeat and understand each instruction.	Look for comfort by waiting for your muscles to soften, not through shifting.

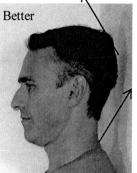

40. Allow your back to settle against the wall. Since there is no book, your head will not touch anything. Do not pull your head back or forward.

Better   Worse

40. Walking away from the wall, let your pelvis be the last part of you touching the wall.

Better

Worse

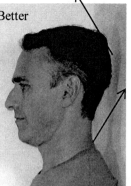

Better

42. Head releasing forward and up.

Worse

42. Head pulled down and back, shortening the spine.

42. Your spine reaches all the way to the level of your ears, higher than the roof of your mouth. As you allow your neck to soften, your head will rise a little, giving more room to your spine.

Head releasing from pointing spine.

44. Easily point the top of your spine as if you were pointing your finger. Avoid trying to straighten the curves of the spine. The curves give the spine some of the qualities of a spring.

Exhale

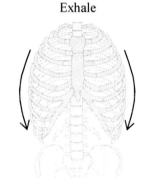

Inhale

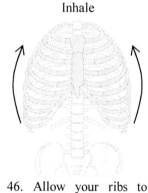

46. Allow your ribs to swing freely from your pointing spine in response to your breathing.

The Shoulders

Whether standing or sitting, it is very common for people to pull their shoulders forward and together, causing the chest to narrow and the back to round. The answer is not to pull the shoulders back, but to stop pulling them together and forward. Holding your shoulders back can make your chest wider, but it also makes your back narrower and impinges arm movement. Sometimes people pull their shoulders up. Again, the answer is not to push them down but to stop pulling them up. There is no need to "hold" your shoulders anywhere. Optimally, your shoulders should rest on top of your hanging ribs, gently pointing away from each other like your pointing spine.

Part III, Section 6. Allow Your Feet to Become Free From Your Ankles

After practicing Parts I and II, gently stand up and lean your torso against a wall, including your pelvis but not your head. Imagine that leaning is as easy as lying down. Avoid moving around in order to look for the best position. Without pushing, allow your back to rest against the wall (there will be some gaps between your back and the wall). Leave your eyes open. With your mind's eye, look for the top of your spine, somewhere about the level of your ears and higher than the roof of your mouth. As your torso settles back, gently allow your head to become free from the top of your spine, as if it were resting on the book. Continuing to release your head from the top of your spine, gently point the top of your spine as if it were reaching past the back of your head.

Allow your ribs to hang softly from your pointing spine as you notice their effortless movement (front, sides, and back) in response to your breathing. Without pushing, allow your shoulders to drift toward the wall as you gently point them away from each other. Allow for widening across your whole torso, front and back, as you continue to allow your hanging ribs to move effortlessly on your pointing spine.

Allow your ankles to soften so that your heels can gently rotate into the floor.

When you are ready to end the exercise, bring your feet together and step backwards until your heels touch the wall. As you take your first step away from the wall, let your pelvis be the last part of you touching the wall. Be aware of your surroundings and leave the exercise until the next time.

Allow your heels to rotate gently into the floor.

Remain open to new discoveries every time you practice the exercise.	Don't rush. Give yourself plenty of time to repeat and understand each instruction.	Look for comfort by waiting for your muscles to soften, not through shifting.

Better

Head releasing from pointing spine.

40. Allow your back to settle against the wall. Since there is no book, your head will not touch anything. Do not pull your head back or forward.

Better   Worse

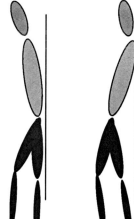

40. Walking away from the wall, let your pelvis be the last part of you touching the wall.

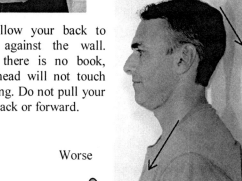

Worse

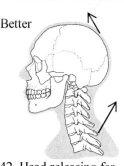

Better

42. Head releasing forward and up.

Worse

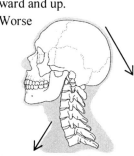

42. Head pulled down and back, shortening the spine.

42. Your spine reaches all the way to the level of your ears, higher than the roof of your mouth. As you allow your neck to soften, your head will rise a little, giving more room to your spine.

44. Easily point the top of your spine as if you were pointing your finger. Avoid trying to straighten the curves of the spine. The curves give the spine some of the qualities of a spring.

Exhale

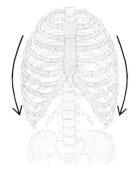

Inhale

46. Allow your ribs to swing freely from your pointing spine in response to your breathing.

48. Gently point your shoulders away from each other.

Ankles, Feet, and Legs

As you allow your ankles to soften, your feet will be able to become free from your legs. This will give you a sense that your legs are a little longer. And as your ankles soften, you might notice your heels' ability to rotate a little more fully into the floor.

www.freeyourneck.com

Part III, Section 7. Allow Your Legs to Lengthen

After practicing Parts I and II, gently stand up and lean your torso against a wall, including your pelvis but not your head. Imagine that leaning is as easy as lying down. Avoid moving around in order to look for the best position. Without pushing, allow your back to rest against the wall (there will be some gaps between your back and the wall). Leave your eyes open. With your mind's eye, look for the top of your spine, somewhere about the level of your ears and higher than the roof of your mouth. As your torso settles back, gently allow your head to become free from the top of your spine, as if it were resting on the book. Continuing to release your head from the top of your spine, gently point the top of your spine as if it were reaching past the back of your head.

Allow your ribs to hang softly from your pointing spine as you notice their effortless movement (front, sides, and back) in response to your breathing. Without pushing, allow your shoulders to drift toward the wall as you gently point them away from each other. Allow for widening across your whole torso, front and back, as you continue to allow your hanging ribs to move effortlessly on your pointing spine.

Allow your ankles to soften so that your heels can gently rotate into the floor. **As your feet become free from your ankles, think of your legs as lengthening from your feet up as if your legs are hanging from your torso.**

When you are ready to end the exercise, bring your feet together and step backwards until your heels touch the wall. As you take your first step away from the wall, let your pelvis be the last part of you touching the wall. Be aware of your surroundings and leave the exercise until the next time.

While leaning against the wall, avoid trying to pull your feet toward you. Think of your legs as reaching to the floor from your feet up.

Remain open to new discoveries every time you practice the exercise.	Don't rush. Give yourself plenty of time to repeat and understand each instruction.	Look for comfort by waiting for your muscles to soften, not through shifting.

40. Allow your back to settle against the wall. Since there is no book, your head will not touch anything. Do not pull your head back or forward.

Better   Worse

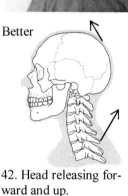

40. Walking away from the wall, let your pelvis be the last part of you touching the wall.

Better

Worse

42. Head releasing forward and up.

Worse

42. Head pulled down and back, shortening the spine.

42. Your spine reaches all the way to the level of your ears, higher than the roof of your mouth. As you allow your neck to soften, your head will rise a little, giving more room to your spine.

Head releasing from pointing spine.

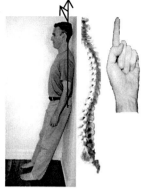

44. Easily point the top of your spine as if you were pointing your finger. Avoid trying to straighten the curves of the spine. The curves give the spine some of the qualities of a spring.

Exhale

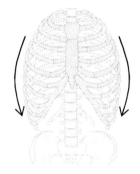

Inhale

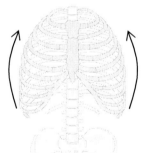

46. Allow your ribs to swing freely from your pointing spine in response to your breathing.

48. Gently point your shoulders away from each other.

Legs Lengthening

Leaning against the wall, you might imagine that the wall is partially supporting you. To feel a little taller, try imagining that your whole torso, everything above your legs, is supported by the wall so that you might feel as though your legs are hanging off you. Think of your legs as reaching toward the floor from your feet, up.

50. Allow your heels to rotate gently into the floor.

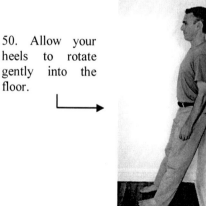

www.freeyourneck.com

Part III, Section 8. Allow Your Whole Torso to Rise above Your Legs

After practicing Parts I and II, gently stand up and lean your torso against a wall, including your pelvis but not your head. Imagine that leaning is as easy as lying down. Avoid moving around in order to look for the best position. Without pushing, allow your back to rest against the wall (there will be some gaps between your back and the wall). Leave your eyes open. With your mind's eye, look for the top of your spine, somewhere about the level of your ears and higher than the roof of your mouth. As your torso settles back, gently allow your head to become free from the top of your spine, as if it were resting on the book. Continuing to release your head from the top of your spine, gently point the top of your spine as if it were reaching past the back of your head.

Allow your ribs to hang softly from your pointing spine as you notice their effortless movement (front, sides, and back) in response to your breathing. Without pushing, allow your shoulders to drift toward the wall as you gently point them away from each other. Allow for widening across your whole torso, front and back, as you continue to allow your hanging ribs to move effortlessly on your pointing spine.

Allow your ankles to soften so that your heels can gently rotate into the floor. As your feet become free from your ankles, think of your legs as lengthening from your feet up as if your legs are hanging from your torso.

Think of your whole upper body as though it were rising from the top down to your pelvis and as though it were suspended above your hanging legs.

When you are ready to end the exercise, bring your feet together and step backwards until your heels touch the wall. As you take your first step away from the wall, let your pelvis be the last part of you touching the wall. Be aware of your surroundings and leave the exercise until the next time.

Think of your whole torso as suspended above your lengthening legs.

Remain open to new discoveries every time you practice the exercise.	Don't rush. Give yourself plenty of time to repeat and understand each instruction.	Look for comfort by waiting for your muscles to soften, not through shifting.

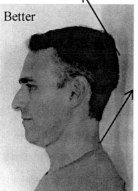

40. Allow your back to settle against the wall. Since there is no book, your head will not touch anything. Do not pull your head back or forward.

Better   Worse

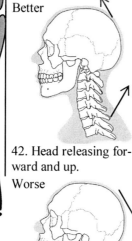

40. Walking away from the wall, let your pelvis be the last part of you touching the wall.

Better

Worse

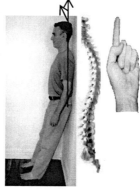

Better

42. Head releasing forward and up.

Worse

42. Head pulled down and back, shortening the spine.

42. Your spine reaches all the way to the level of your ears, higher than the roof of your mouth. As you allow your neck to soften, your head will rise a little, giving more room to your spine.

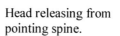
Head releasing from pointing spine.

44. Easily point the top of your spine as if you were pointing your finger. Avoid trying to straighten the curves of the spine. The curves give the spine some of the qualities of a spring.

Exhale

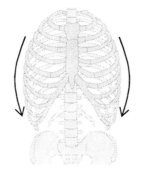

Inhale

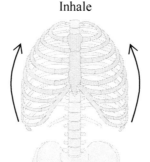

46. Allow your ribs to swing freely from your pointing spine in response to your breathing.

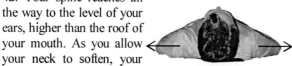

48. Gently point your shoulders away from each other.

Feeling Lighter

Some of your feeling of how heavy you are is based on your perception. If you think of yourself as light, you might feel lighter and you might be able to move as if you were lighter. This culminating section gives you a chance to change your perception of how heavy you are.

If your legs are lengthening as they reach to the floor from the bottom up, and your torso is lengthening as the top of your spine points up as if it were reaching past the back of your head, maybe you will be able to find some separation in the middle, as if your torso were suspended a bit above your legs. As you consider this idea, remember to allow your spine to point up without lifting your ribs or pulling in your stomach.

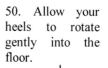
50. Allow your heels to rotate gently into the floor.

52. Avoid trying to pull your feet toward you. Think of your legs as reaching to the floor from your feet up.

      www.freeyourneck.com

Part III, Section 9. Part III in Full

After practicing Parts I and II, gently stand up and lean your torso against a wall, including your pelvis but not your head. Imagine that leaning is as easy as lying down. Avoid moving around in order to look for the best position. Without pushing, allow your back to rest against the wall (there will be some gaps between your back and the wall). Leave your eyes open. With your mind's eye, look for the top of your spine, somewhere about the level of your ears and higher than the roof of your mouth. As your torso settles back, gently allow your head to become free from the top of your spine, as if it were resting on the book. Continuing to release your head from the top of your spine, gently point the top of your spine as if it were reaching past the back of your head.

Allow your ribs to hang softly from your pointing spine as you notice their effortless movement (front, sides, and back) in response to your breathing. Without pushing, allow your shoulders to drift toward the wall as you gently point them away from each other. Allow for widening across your whole torso, front and back, as you continue to allow your hanging ribs to move effortlessly on your pointing spine.

Allow your ankles to soften so that your heels can gently rotate into the floor. As your feet become free from your ankles, think of your legs as lengthening from your feet up as if your legs are hanging from your torso.

Think of your whole upper body as though it were rising from the top down to your pelvis and as though it were suspended above your hanging legs.

When you are ready to end the exercise, bring your feet together and step backwards until your heels touch the wall. As you take your first step away from the wall, let your pelvis be the last part of you touching the wall. Be aware of your surroundings and leave the exercise until the next time.

Remain open to new discoveries every time you practice the exercise.	Don't rush. Give yourself plenty of time to repeat and understand each instruction.	Look for comfort by waiting for your muscles to soften, not through shifting.

Better

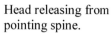

Head releasing from pointing spine.

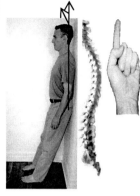

Part III Summary

I hope that now you feel a little bit longer and lighter as you lean against the wall. The next step is allowing for the same feeling of length and lightness as you become more active by moving and bending. Remember, even the smallest difference in how you feel or perceive yourself can be beneficial. And your good feeling can grow.

40. Allow your back to settle against the wall. Since there is no book, your head will not touch anything. Do not pull your head back or forward.

Better   Worse

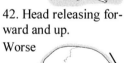

44. Easily point the top of your spine as if you were pointing your finger. Avoid trying to straighten the curves of the spine. The curves give the spine some of the qualities of a spring.

50. Allow your heels to rotate gently into the floor.

Worse

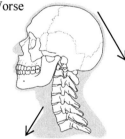

Exhale

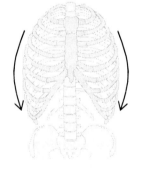

40. Walking away from the wall, let your pelvis be the last part of you touching the wall.

Better

42. Head releasing forward and up.

Worse

42. Head pulled down and back, shortening the spine.

Inhale

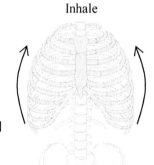

46. Allow your ribs to swing freely from your pointing spine in response to your breathing.

52. Avoid trying to pull your feet toward you. Think of your legs as reaching to the floor from your feet up.

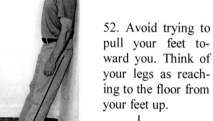

42. Your spine reaches all the way to the level of your ears, higher than the roof of your mouth. As you allow your neck to soften, your head will rise a little, giving more room to your spine.

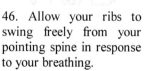

48. Gently point your shoulders away from each other.

54. Think of your whole torso as suspended above your lengthening legs.

Part IV

Bending in a Semi-Vertical Position

Before You Begin

This fourth part of the exercise uses a semi-vertical position to re-discover the same extra room within your body while moving. In this part, you will bend both knees at the same time as you notice your torso stays against and slides down the wall. As the exercise moves on you will bend the torso forward, using the hip joints and not the smaller joints of the spine.

Bending the torso forward by bending the spine (i.e. bending at the waist) shortens your spine, impedes breathing, and results in a weaker final position. Repeatedly bending from the waist, especially when lifting something, can also damage the spine. By relying on the hip, knee, and ankle joints in order to lower yourself toward the floor, while at the same time allowing for the same length and width of your torso, your ability to bend will become easier, stronger, and more graceful.

The end of Part III will leave you ready to begin the three sections of Part IV seamlessly with your torso leaning against a wall. The activity for Part IV, virtually the same as Part II except in a semi-vertical position, is to **discover the same conditions that you are establishing throughout the exercise** while leaning against the wall and bending your knees. Your objective is to avoid compromising the release of your head and ribs from your pointing spine (all the work you have been doing so far) for the sake of the movement. **The movement is always secondary to allowing for room as you move.**

Every time, before you practice Part IV, practice Parts I through III first. Spend 1–5 minutes on this part of the exercise (more if you like) but remember that you do not need to lengthen the amount of time you spend on the whole exercise.

As you practice the exercise, you may discover a subtle difference in how you experience your body. Try to remain open to new discoveries every time. When you walk away from the wall, do it slowly and easily. Be aware of your surroundings and leave the exercise until the next time you practice it.

Equipment

A smooth wall with no obstructions from the floor to your full height and width, and clothing that can slide easily along the wall. Your feet can be bare or you can wear shoes as long as your feet are not able to slide on the floor.

www.freeyourneck.com

Part IV, Section 1. Bend Your Knees without Shortening or Narrowing

After practicing parts I through III, **leaning against the wall—your head releasing from the top of your spine, your spine pointing up, your ribs softening, without disturbing the relationship between your head and spine—and keeping your pelvis against the wall, slowly bend your knees, making sure that your knees point in the same direction as your feet.**

When you are ready to end the exercise, **without disturbing the relationship between your head and spine, reverse the previous process and slowly press the floor away with your feet so that your legs straighten, causing your torso to slide up along the wall as it also stays against the wall.** Bring your feet together and step backwards until your heels are against the wall. As you take your first step away from the wall, let your pelvis be the last part of you touching the wall. Be aware of your surroundings and leave the exercise until the next time.

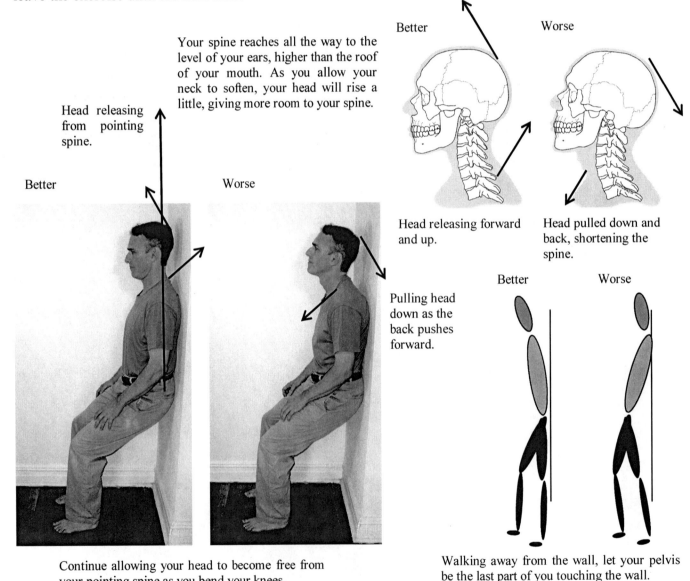

Your spine reaches all the way to the level of your ears, higher than the roof of your mouth. As you allow your neck to soften, your head will rise a little, giving more room to your spine.

Head releasing from pointing spine.

Better

Worse

Better

Worse

Head releasing forward and up.

Head pulled down and back, shortening the spine.

Pulling head down as the back pushes forward.

Better

Worse

Continue allowing your head to become free from your pointing spine as you bend your knees.

Walking away from the wall, let your pelvis be the last part of you touching the wall.

Remain open to new discoveries every time you practice the exercise.	Don't rush. Give yourself plenty of time to repeat and understand each instruction.	Look for comfort by waiting for your muscles to soften, not through shifting.

Bending Your Knees

You've been doing it all your life and it may seem obviously simple, but bending your knees while standing is one of the most coordinationally demanding movements that your body does. Bending the knees causes a cascade of muscular and joint responses that should generally include movement at the hip and ankle joints.

Because the movement is complicated, it often includes misplaced joint movement and muscle use. Leaning against the wall makes using the proper joints a little simpler, but be very careful to maintain the conditions: your head releasing from the top of your spine, your spine pointing, your ribs softening and all the rest of the work you are doing to find more room within your body.

Part IV, Section 2. Bend Forward at the Hip without Shortening or Narrowing

After practicing parts I through III, leaning against the wall, your head releasing from the top of your spine, your spine pointing up, your ribs softening, without disturbing the relationship between your head and spine, and keeping your pelvis against the wall, slowly bend your knees, making sure that your knees point in the same direction as your feet. **Leaving your knees bent while continuing to point your spine and without disturbing the relationship between your head and your spine, as if the wall were tilting, slowly bend forward at the hip. Notice your pelvis rotating against the wall as you move.**

When you are ready to end the exercise, without disturbing the relationship between your head and spine, **reverse the previous process and slowly rotate your torso from your hip joints back to the wall,** press the floor away with your feet so that your legs straighten, causing your torso to slide up the wall as it also stays against the wall. Bring your feet together and step backwards until your heels are against the wall. As you take your first step away from the wall, let your pelvis be the last part of you touching the wall. Be aware of your surroundings and leave the exercise until the next time.

Head releasing from pointing spine.

Continue allowing your head to become free from your pointing spine as you bend at the hip.

Better

Worse

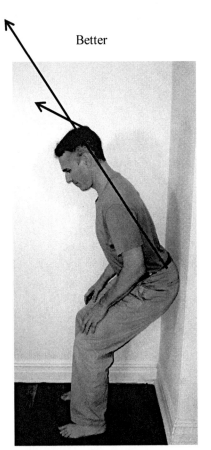
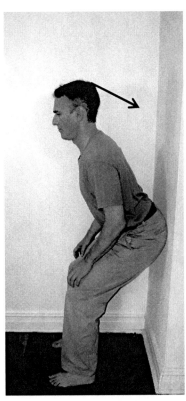

Remain open to new discoveries every time you practice the exercise.	Don't rush. Give yourself plenty of time to repeat and understand each instruction.	Look for comfort by waiting for your muscles to soften, not through shifting.

www.freeyourneck.com

Head releasing from pointing spine.

Better

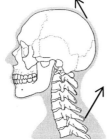

Better

60. Head releasing forward and up.

Worse

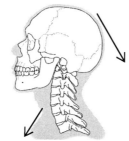

60. Head pulled down and back, shortening the spine.

Leaving Your Neck behind Your Head

As you bend forward, be absolutely certain that you are only bending at the hip joints. You should be able to feel your pelvis rotating on the wall. Leave your torso the same as if it were still leaning against the wall and avoid pulling your head back and down.

60. Your spine reaches all the way to the level of your ears, higher than the roof of your mouth. As you allow your neck to soften, your head will rise a little, giving more room to your spine.

Worse

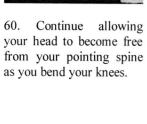

60. Continue allowing your head to become free from your pointing spine as you bend your knees.

Better   Worse

60. Walking away from the wall, let your pelvis be the last part of you touching the wall.

Part IV, Section 3. Part IV in Full

After practicing parts I through III, leaning against the wall, your head releasing from the top of your spine, your spine pointing up, your ribs softening, without disturbing the relationship between your head and spine, and keeping your pelvis against the wall, slowly bend your knees, making sure that your knees point in the same direction as your feet. Leaving your knees bent while continuing to point your spine and without disturbing the relationship between your head and your spine, as if the wall were tilting, slowly bend forward at the hip. Notice your pelvis rotating against the wall as you move.

When you are ready to end the exercise, without disturbing the relationship between your head and spine, reverse the previous process and slowly rotate your torso from your hip joints back to the wall, press the floor away with your feet so that your legs straighten, causing your torso to slide up the wall as it also stays against the wall. Bring your feet together and step backwards until your heels are against the wall. As you take your first step away from the wall, let your pelvis be the last part of you touching the wall. Be aware of your surroundings and leave the exercise until the next time.

Remain open to new discoveries every time you practice the exercise.	Don't rush. Give yourself plenty of time to repeat and understand each instruction.	Look for comfort by waiting for your muscles to soften, not through shifting.

Head releasing from pointing spine.

Better

Better

Worse

60. Continue allowing your head to become free from your pointing spine as you bend your knees.

Better

60. Head releasing forward and up.

Worse

60. Head pulled down and back, shortening the spine.

60. Your spine reaches all the way to the level of your ears, higher than the roof of your mouth. As you allow your neck to soften, your head will rise a little, giving more room to your spine.

Better   Worse

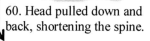

60. Walking away from the wall, let your pelvis be the last part of you touching the wall.

62. Head releasing from pointing spine.

Better

Worse

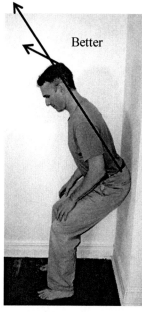

62. Continue allowing your head to become free from your pointing spine as you bend at the hip.

Part IV Summary

I hope that by now you are beginning to discover some of the extra room within your body as you are lying down and that you are able to discover that same quality within your body as you transfer to standing in a semi-vertical position. You are almost ready to take the exercise into standing on your own and finally discovering greater ease, comfort, and poise every moment of your life.

So far, much of the exercise has been purposefully repetitious. All of the work you have done will continue to be useful, but now, you will be asked to add another component to your awareness. The physical actions will remain the same but you are going to look at them a little differently.

Part V

Your Torso Always Goes Up

Before You Begin

This fifth part of the exercise examines something new, using the inherent "oppositional relationship" between your legs and your torso. So far you have been looking for more room within your body. This may not be too difficult when lying down, or even in the semi-vertical position, but when you start standing and moving, lifting and bending, finding this extra room becomes much more difficult unless you use this oppositional relationship within your body.

The end of Part IV will leave you ready to begin the six sections of Part V seamlessly with your back leaning against a wall. The activity for Part V is a little different from previous activities. Although the movements and the primacy of maintaining space are virtually the same as in Parts II and IV, you will also be asked to observe the oppositional relationship between your legs and torso. **The movement will also be secondary to discovering and using this oppositional relationship.**

Every time, before you practice Part V, practice Parts I through IV first. Spend 1–5 minutes on Part V (more if you like) but remember that you do not need to lengthen the amount of time you spend on the whole exercise.

As you practice the exercise, you may discover a subtle difference in how you experience your body. Try to remain open to new discoveries every time. When you walk away from the wall, do it slowly and easily. Be aware of your surroundings and leave the exercise until the next time you practice it.

Equipment

A smooth wall with no obstructions from the floor to your full height, and clothing that can slide easily along the wall. Your feet can be bare or you can wear shoes as long as your feet are not able to slide on the floor.

Part V, Section 1. Notice Your Feet Going Forward and Down toward the Floor

After practicing Parts I–IV—your spine pointing, head releasing, ribs softening—**notice that your feet and legs are going forward and down into the floor so that they would slide away if the floor were slippery.**

When you are ready to end the exercise, without disturbing the relationship between your head and spine, bring your feet together and step backwards until your heels are against the wall. As you take your first step away from the wall, let your pelvis be the last part of you touching the wall. Be aware of your surroundings and leave the exercise until the next time.

Your legs are going forward and down.

Better   Worse

Walking away from the wall, let your pelvis be the last part of you touching the wall.

Remain open to new discoveries every time you practice the exercise.	Don't rush. Give yourself plenty of time to repeat and understand each instruction.	Look for comfort by waiting for your muscles to soften, not through shifting.

www.freeyourneck.com   ©2010 Leland Vall

Where Are Your Legs Going?

While leaning against the wall, without doing anything else, you can recognize that your feet and legs are pressing forward and down against the floor. You can tell that they are doing this because if not for the friction between your feet and the floor, your feet would slide away and you would fall down.

In effect, your legs are engaged in keeping your upper body away from the floor.

www.freeyourneck.com

Part V, Section 2. Notice That Your Torso Is Going Back and Up

After practicing Parts I–IV—your spine pointing, head releasing, ribs softening—notice that your feet and legs are going forward and down into the floor so that they would slide away if the floor were slippery. **Notice also that your whole torso is going backward and upward toward the wall so that it would fall backwards if the wall gave way.**

When you are ready to end the exercise, without disturbing the relationship between your head and spine, bring your feet together and step backwards until your heels are against the wall. As you take your first step away from the wall, let your pelvis be the last part of you touching the wall. Be aware of your surroundings and leave the exercise until the next time.

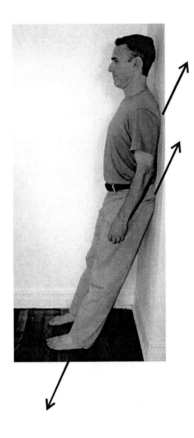

Your torso is going up and back.

Your legs are going forward and down.

Remain open to new discoveries every time you practice the exercise.	Don't rush. Give yourself plenty of time to repeat and understand each instruction.	Look for comfort by waiting for your muscles to soften, not through shifting.

68. Your legs are going forward and down.

Where Is Your Torso Going?

If your legs are going forward and down into the floor, then your whole torso must be pressing back and up into the wall. You can tell that this is happening because if the wall were weak, your back would push through the wall.

Finding the Opposition

Without having to work at it, you can notice that there is an opposition going on between your legs and your back. Your legs are going forward and down toward the floor and your torso is going up and back toward the wall.

Better   Worse

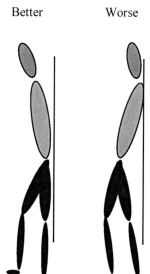

68. Walking away from the wall, let your pelvis be the last part of you touching the wall.

     www.freeyourneck.com

Part V, Section 3. Keep the Ground Away from You While Bending Your Knees

After practicing Parts I–IV—your spine pointing, head releasing, ribs softening—notice that your feet and legs are going forward and down into the floor so that they would slide away if the floor were slippery. Notice also that your whole torso is going backward and upward toward the wall so that it would fall backwards if the wall gave way.

Leaning your whole torso against the wall and continuing to point your spine, release your head and allow your ribs to soften; bend your knees while also noticing that you are not pulling the ground toward you. Notice that even though your torso is closer to the ground, your legs are still oriented down and forward toward the ground.

When you are ready to end the exercise, without disturbing the relationship between your head and spine, reverse the previous process and slowly press the floor away with your feet so that your legs straighten, bring your feet together and step backwards until your heels are against the wall. As you take your first step away from the wall, let your pelvis be the last part of you touching the wall. Be aware of your surroundings and leave the exercise until the next time.

Even as you bend your knees, your legs are going down toward the floor and your torso is going up.

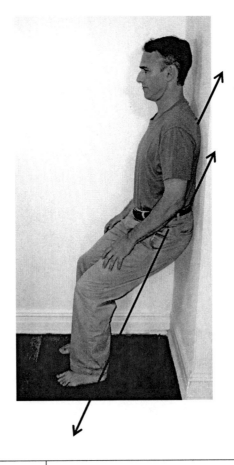

Remain open to new discoveries every time you practice the exercise.	Don't rush. Give yourself plenty of time to repeat and understand each instruction.	Look for comfort by waiting for your muscles to soften, not through shifting.

70. Your torso is going up and back.

68. Your legs are going forward and down.

70. Your legs are going forward and down.

The Ground Is Down, Your Torso Is Up

Notice that even though you are getting closer to the floor, you are not pulling the floor closer to you. Your feet are still going down toward the floor. You are still keeping the floor away from you even as you bend your knees. **Even though your knees are bending you are still, in effect, standing up just as you were before bending your knees.**

Although it may be difficult at first, this is an important concept to understand. As long as your feet are on the ground and your legs are supporting you, no matter how bent your knees, you are still standing as if you were standing with straight legs.

Better   Worse

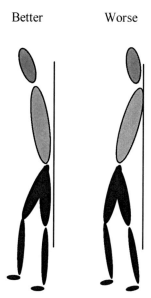

68. Walking away from the wall, let your pelvis be the last part of you touching the wall.

Part V, Section 4. The Torso Goes Back and Up Even As It Is Forward

After practicing Parts I–IV—your spine pointing, head releasing, ribs softening—notice that your feet and legs are going forward and down into the floor so that they would slide away if the floor were slippery. Notice also that your whole torso is going backward and upward toward the wall so that it would fall backwards if the wall gave way.

Leaning your whole torso against the wall and continuing to point your spine, release your head and allow your ribs to soften; bend your knees while also noticing that you are not pulling the ground toward you. Notice that even though your torso is closer to the ground, your legs are still oriented down and forward toward the ground.

Continuing to point your spine, to release your head, and to allow your ribs to soften, rotate your torso forward at the hip joint while recognizing that you are actually resisting the force of gravity that is pulling you down.

When you are ready to end the exercise, without disturbing the relationship between your head and spine, rotate your back from the hip joints back to the wall, straighten your legs, bring your feet together and step backwards until your heels are against the wall. As you take your first step away from the wall, let your pelvis be the last part of you touching the wall. Be aware of your surroundings and leave the exercise until the next time.

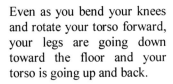

Even as you bend your knees and rotate your torso forward, your legs are going down toward the floor and your torso is going up and back.

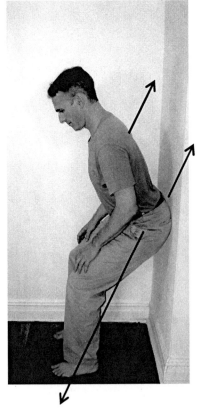

Remain open to new discoveries every time you practice the exercise.	Don't rush. Give yourself plenty of time to repeat and understand each instruction.	Look for comfort by waiting for your muscles to soften, not through shifting.

70. Your torso is going up and back.

68. Your legs are going forward and down.

70. Your legs are going forward and down.

Your Forward Torso Is Still Back

As you rotate your torso forward, you might think that this forward movement is what you are doing but you can also think just the opposite. As your torso rotates forward from the hip, its tendency to fall towards the floor becomes greater. In response to this, the muscles in your back automatically activate to prevent your torso from falling over. Your torso is heavy and as it tips forward, you have to hold it back and up.

In the exercise, as your torso rotates forward, recognize that you are resisting the force of gravity. You can also imagine that the wall is tilting forward and that you are resisting that force as your torso rotates forward.

Thinking this way might be counterintuitive but it is actually closer to what is going on. You are not going down, you are going up.

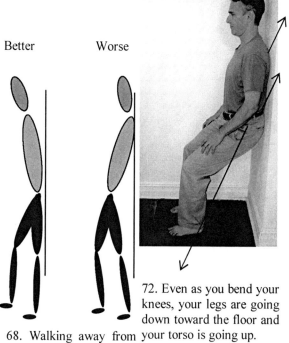

Better   Worse

72. Even as you bend your knees, your legs are going down toward the floor and your torso is going up.

68. Walking away from the wall, let your pelvis be the last part of you touching the wall.

Part V, Section 5. Re-Defining Bending at the Hip and Knees

After practicing Parts I–IV—your spine pointing, head releasing, ribs softening—notice that your feet and legs are going forward and down into the floor so that they would slide away if the floor were slippery. Notice also that your whole torso is going backward and upward toward the wall so that it would fall backwards if the wall gave way.

Leaning your whole torso against the wall and continuing to point your spine, release your head and allow your ribs to soften; bend your knees while also noticing that you are not pulling the ground toward you. Notice that even though your torso is closer to the ground, your legs are still oriented down and forward toward the ground.

Continuing to point your spine, to release your head, and to allow your ribs to soften, rotate your torso forward at the hip joint while recognizing that you are actually resisting the force of gravity that is pulling you down.

Remain here for a moment and imagine that you are effortlessly supporting 100 pounds on your back. Even though your back is forward in space, notice that it is still oriented back and up in relation to your legs and that your legs are still oriented forward and down in relation to your back.

When you are ready to end the exercise, without disturbing the relationship between your head and spine rotate your back from the hip joints back to the wall, straighten your legs, bring your feet together and step backwards until your heels are against the wall. As you take your first step away from the wall, let your pelvis be the last part of you touching the wall. Be aware of your surroundings and leave the exercise until the next time.

Even as you bend your knees and rotate your torso forward, your legs are going down toward the floor and your torso is going up.

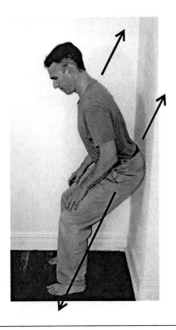

Remain open to new discoveries every time you practice the exercise.	Don't rush. Give yourself plenty of time to repeat and understand each instruction.	Look for comfort by waiting for your muscles to soften, not through shifting.

www.freeyourneck.com

70. Your torso is going up and back.

68. Your legs are going forward and down.

70. Your legs are going forward and down.

If Your Feet Are on the Floor, You Are Standing

Compare this new position to the way you started Part V. It is easy to notice that even though your knees are bent, your legs are still keeping you up and away from the floor. You are still standing.

At the same time, your torso isn't really going forward because you are certainly more concerned about keeping your torso up and away from the floor. Your torso is still up and back.

With your legs still going down and forward toward the floor and your torso still going up and back toward the wall, this new position is not very different from your original position leaning against the wall.

Even in this new position, your legs and feet are still going forward and down and your torso is still going back and up. You are still going up.

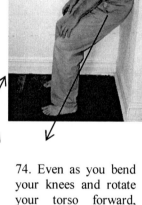

74. Even as you bend your knees and rotate your torso forward, your legs are going down toward the floor and your torso is going up and back.

Better   Worse

72. Even as you bend your knees, your legs are going down toward the floor and your torso is going up.

68. Walking away from the wall, let your pelvis be the last part of you touching the wall.

Part V, Section 6. Part V in Full

After practicing Parts I–IV—your spine pointing, head releasing, ribs softening—notice that your feet and legs are going forward and down into the floor so that they would slide away if the floor were slippery. Notice also that your whole torso is going backward and upward toward the wall so that it would fall backwards if the wall gave way.

Leaning your whole torso against the wall and continuing to point your spine, release your head and allow your ribs to soften; bend your knees while also noticing that you are not pulling the ground toward you. Notice that even though your torso is closer to the ground, your legs are still oriented down and forward toward the ground.

Continuing to point your spine, to release your head, and to allow your ribs to soften, rotate your torso forward at the hip joint while recognizing that you are actually resisting the force of gravity that is pulling you down.

Remain here for a moment and imagine that you are effortlessly supporting 100 pounds on your back. Even though your back is forward in space, notice that it is still oriented back and up in relation to your legs and that your legs are still oriented forward and down in relation to your back.

When you are ready to end the exercise, without disturbing the relationship between your head and spine rotate your back from the hip joints back to the wall, straighten your legs, bring your feet together and step backwards until your heels are against the wall. As you take your first step away from the wall, let your pelvis be the last part of you touching the wall. Be aware of your surroundings and leave the exercise until the next time.

Remain open to new discoveries every time you practice the exercise.	Don't rush. Give yourself plenty of time to repeat and understand each instruction.	Look for comfort by waiting for your muscles to soften, not through shifting.

70. Your torso is going up and back.

68. Your legs are going forward and down.

70. Your legs are going forward and down.

Part V Summary

Generally, when people bend, they pull themselves toward the floor. This action pulls the body together, making it smaller and also making the movement more difficult and less effective.

As you approach the floor in this part of the exercise, think that you are really keeping yourself away from the floor and maintaining the same conditions for standing. Thinking in this way while bending will make the movement stronger, more stable, and easier to accomplish. It will also look better.

In this part of the exercise, you lean against a wall in order to make the lesson clearer and the movement physically easier. In Part VI, you will begin to work without the wall.

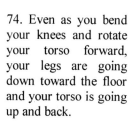

74. Even as you bend your knees and rotate your torso forward, your legs are going down toward the floor and your torso is going up and back.

Better   Worse

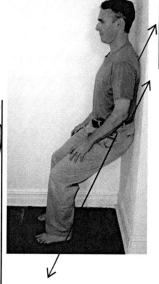

72. Even as you bend your knees, your legs are going down toward the floor and your torso is going up.

68. Walking away from the wall, let your pelvis be the last part of you touching the wall.

www.freeyourneck.com

Part VI

Standing and Bending

Before You Begin

The sixth part of the exercise is the culmination of the five previous parts and it illustrates how all those skills apply to standing and moving with greater ease and poise. For the first time you will specifically apply the instructions from the exercise while you are standing and bending on your own away from the wall.

The end of Part V will leave you ready to begin the six sections of Part VI seamlessly with your torso leaning against a wall. The activity for Part VI, virtually the same as all the previous parts of the exercise except that it is performed free-standing, is to **discover the same conditions that you are establishing throughout the exercise** as you stand and bend on your own. Your objective is to avoid compromising your pointing spine, the release of your head from the top of your spine, your softening ribs, and all the work you are doing, for the sake of the movement. **The movement is always secondary to allowing for room as you move.**

Every time, before you practice Part VI, practice Parts I through V first. Then spend 1–5 minutes on Part VI (more if you like) but remember that you do not need to lengthen the amount of time you spend on the whole exercise.

As you practice the exercise, you may discover a subtle difference in how you experience your body. Try to remain open to new discoveries every time. When you are ready to finish the exercise, just walk away. Be aware of your surroundings and leave the exercise until the next time you practice it.

Equipment

A smooth wall with no obstructions from the floor to your full height, and clothing that can slide easily along the wall. Your feet can be bare or you can wear shoes as long as your feet are not able to slide on the floor.

www.freeyourneck.com

Part VI, Section 1. Prepare to Walk Away from the Wall

After practicing Parts I–V, **while still leaning against the wall, your spine pointing, head releasing from the top of your spine, ribs softening, and continuing to develop all the previous conditions, bring your feet together and walk backwards until your heels touch the wall. As your feet walk backwards, be careful not to let your head drift back with them.**

With your heels against the wall, recognize that although you are no longer leaning, your legs are still in opposition to your torso. Your legs are still going forward and down toward the floor and your whole torso, from the pelvis up, is still going back and up toward the wall.

When you are ready to walk away from the wall, as you take your first step, let your pelvis be the last part of you touching the wall. Be aware of your surroundings and leave the exercise until the next time.

Remain open to new discoveries every time you practice the exercise.	Don't rush. Give yourself plenty of time to repeat and understand each instruction.	Look for comfort by waiting for your muscles to soften, not through shifting.

Thinking Back

In a moment you will walk away from the wall. This is the moment when you will begin to have an opportunity to recognize that all the work you are doing in the exercise applies to all the standing, bending, and moving that you do in your regular life.

To begin taking advantage of this opportunity you will need to set aside, at least during the exercise, much of how you conceive standing and bending and rely on the exercise and on what you have learned through the exercise so far.

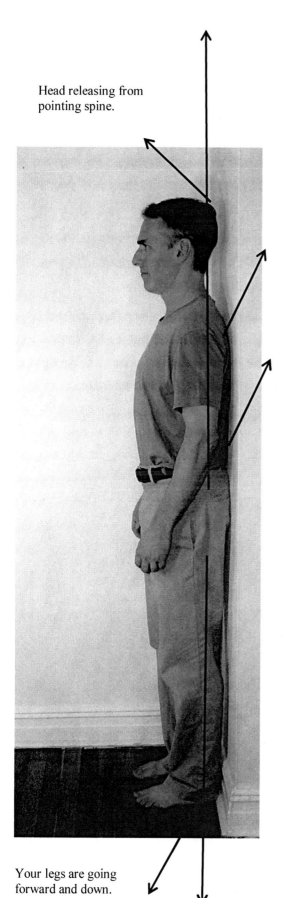

Head releasing from pointing spine.

Your back is going back and up.

Your legs are going forward and down.

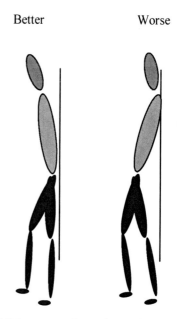

Better   Worse

Walking away from the wall, let your pelvis be the last part of you touching the wall.

Part VI, Section 2. Walk Away from the Wall and Stand Free

After practicing Parts I–V, while still leaning against the wall, your spine pointing, head releasing from the top of your spine, ribs softening, and continuing to develop all the previous conditions, bring your feet together and walk backwards until your heels touch the wall. As your feet walk backwards, be careful not to let your head drift back with them.

With your heels against the wall, recognize that although you are no longer leaning, your legs are still in opposition to your torso. Your legs are still going forward and down toward the floor and your whole torso, from the pelvis up, is still going back and up toward the wall.

Before and as you walk away from the wall, think of your whole torso, from your pelvis up, as continuing to be oriented up and back toward the wall as if the wall were coming with you. Walking away, allow your pelvis to be the last part of your torso touching the wall.

Take a few steps and stop with both feet underneath you. Avoid moving your feet around to settle; just stop. Without leaning back, recognize that your back is still oriented back and up in opposition to your legs which are going forward and down toward the floor. *Allow your torso to be light on your legs as if you were suspended above your legs. Allow your legs to hang from your torso.*

When you are ready to finish the exercise, just walk away. Be aware of your surroundings and leave the exercise until the next time.

Remain open to new discoveries every time you practice the exercise.	Don't rush. Give yourself plenty of time to repeat and understand each instruction.	Look for comfort by waiting for your muscles to soften, not through shifting.

Head releasing from pointing spine.

Your back is going back and up.

Standing on your own, the conditions are still the same.

Your legs are going forward and down.

Bring the Wall with You

As you begin walking away from the wall, avoid pushing the middle of your body out first.

As you walk, think of the experience as something new and allow your torso to be light on your legs as if the wall were still supporting you.

Standing Free

When you are standing upright on your own, there is no longer a need to allow your torso to fall back because there is nothing supporting it. Instead, try just to leave your whole torso behind as you allow your head to release from your pointing spine. Avoid pushing your back forward or pulling your legs backward.

Better

Worse

Walking away from the wall, let your pelvis be the last part of you touching the wall.

Part VI, Section 3. Look for Your Hip Joints

After practicing Parts I–V, while still leaning against the wall, your spine pointing, head releasing from the top of your spine, ribs softening, and continuing to develop all the previous conditions, bring your feet together and walk backwards until your heels touch the wall. As your feet walk backwards, be careful not to let your head drift back with them.

With your heels against the wall, recognize that although you are no longer leaning, your legs are still in opposition to your torso. Your legs are still going forward and down toward the floor and your whole torso, from the pelvis up, is still going back and up toward the wall.

Before and as you walk away from the wall, think of your whole torso, from your pelvis up, as continuing to be oriented up and back toward the wall as if the wall were coming with you. Walking away, allow your pelvis to be the last part of your torso touching the wall.

Take a few steps and stop with both feet underneath you. Avoid moving your feet around to settle; just stop. Without leaning back, recognize that your back is still oriented back and up in opposition to your legs which are going forward and down toward the floor. *Allow your torso to be light on your legs as if you were suspended above your legs. Allow your legs to hang from your torso.*

With one step, bring your feet together. As if your whole torso were still supported by the wall, gently send one knee forward until the heel comes up, send that heel back to the floor and repeat with the other knee, alternately bending each knee five times. Try to minimize the sway of your hips from side to side and avoid any forward movement of your pelvis. Recognize your hip joint at the junction between your legs and pelvis.

When you are ready to finish the exercise, just walk away. Be aware of your surroundings and leave the exercise until the next time.

Remain open to new discoveries every time you practice the exercise.	Don't rush. Give yourself plenty of time to repeat and understand each instruction.	Look for comfort by waiting for your muscles to soften, not through shifting.

Where Is Your Hip Joint?

Continue to observe the difference between your legs and your torso. As you alternately bend your knees, allow your torso to be as still as possible. Try not to let your pelvis rock from side to side or forward and back.

Think of your whole torso as floating a little bit above your legs, allowing your legs to hang freely from your pelvis. With your mind's eye and/or by looking in a mirror, observe what is moving (your legs) and what is staying still (your torso, including your pelvis).

One Step to Bring Your Feet Together

When going from a wide to a narrow stance (or vice versa) try to do it with one clear step without moving your feet around to get them set. Finding the ground is usually as easy as putting your foot down. You don't have to shuffle your feet to find the ground.

Head releasing from pointing spine.

Your back is going back and up.

The knee goes forward, the back stays back. Remember that you are standing as you do this. Because you are standing, it is helpful to think more about the standing leg than the moving leg.

Part VI, Section 4. Bend Both Your Knees

After practicing Parts I–V, while still leaning against the wall, your spine pointing, head releasing from the top of your spine, ribs softening, and continuing to develop all the previous conditions, bring your feet together and walk backwards until your heels touch the wall. As your feet walk backwards, be careful not to let your head drift back with them.

With your heels against the wall, recognize that although you are no longer leaning, your legs are still in opposition to your torso. Your legs are still going forward and down toward the floor and your whole torso, from the pelvis up, is still going back and up toward the wall.

Before and as you walk away from the wall, think of your whole torso, from your pelvis up, as continuing to be oriented up and back toward the wall as if the wall were coming with you. Walking away, allow your pelvis to be the last part of your torso touching the wall.

Take a few steps and stop with both feet underneath you. Avoid moving your feet around to settle; just stop. Without leaning back, recognize that your back is still oriented back and up in opposition to your legs which are going forward and down toward the floor. *Allow your torso to be light on your legs as if you were suspended above your legs. Allow your legs to hang from your torso.*

With one step, bring your feet together. As if your whole torso were still supported by the wall, gently send one knee forward until the heel comes up, send that heel back to the floor and repeat with the other knee, alternately bending each knee five times. Try to minimize the sway of your hips from side to side and avoid any forward movement of your pelvis. Recognize your hip joint at the junction between your legs and pelvis.

While pointing your spine, releasing your head from the top of your spine, and allowing your ribs to soften and your torso to be oriented back and up from your legs, take a wider stance with one step. Gently bend both knees while also recognizing that you are still keeping the floor away from you. Do not allow your pelvis to move forward with your knees and leave your feet flat on the floor as if your legs were still straight.

When you are ready to finish the exercise, **gently press your heels into the floor until your legs straighten. In one step, bring your feet together and just walk away.** Be aware of your surroundings and leave the exercise until the next time.

Remain open to new discoveries every time you practice the exercise.	Don't rush. Give yourself plenty of time to repeat and understand each instruction.	Look for comfort by waiting for your muscles to soften, not through shifting.

Bending Two Knees Is Bending One Twice

Bending both knees is similar to bending one knee. The difference is that when you bend one knee fully, you are still standing, but only on one leg. When you bend both knees, you remain standing on two legs. Remember that as long as at least one foot is fully on the ground, you are always standing up and you are always going up.

One Step to Bring Your Feet Apart

When going from a narrow to a wide stance (or vice versa) try to do it with one clear step without moving your feet around to get them set. Finding the ground is usually as easy as putting your foot down. You don't have to shuffle your feet to find the ground.

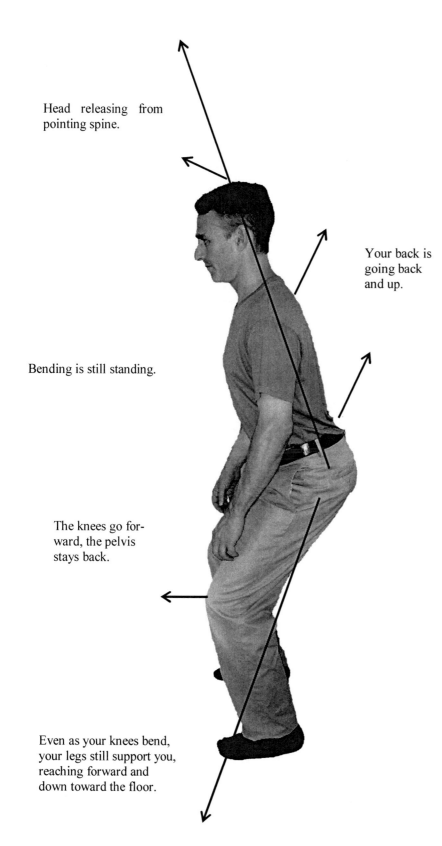

Head releasing from pointing spine.

Your back is going back and up.

Bending is still standing.

The knees go forward, the pelvis stays back.

Even as your knees bend, your legs still support you, reaching forward and down toward the floor.

Part VI, Section 5. Bend Forward from Your Hips

After practicing Parts I–V, while still leaning against the wall, your spine pointing, head releasing from the top of your spine, ribs softening, and continuing to develop all the previous conditions, bring your feet together and walk backwards until your heels touch the wall. As your feet walk backwards, be careful not to let your head drift back with them.

With your heels against the wall, recognize that although you are no longer leaning, your legs are still in opposition to your torso. Your legs are still going forward and down toward the floor and your whole torso, from the pelvis up, is still going back and up toward the wall.

Before and as you walk away from the wall, think of your whole torso, from your pelvis up, as continuing to be oriented up and back toward the wall as if the wall were coming with you. Walking away, allow your pelvis to be the last part of your torso touching the wall.

Take a few steps and stop with both feet underneath you. Avoid moving your feet around to settle; just stop. Without leaning back, recognize that your back is still oriented back and up in opposition to your legs which are going forward and down toward the floor. *Allow your torso to be light on your legs as if you were suspended above your legs. Allow your legs to hang from your torso.*

With one step, bring your feet together. As if your whole torso were still supported by the wall, gently send one knee forward until the heel comes up, send that heel back to the floor and repeat with the other knee, lifting each heel five times. Try to minimize the sway of your hips from side to side and avoid any forward movement of your pelvis. Recognize your hip joint at the junction between your legs and pelvis.

While pointing your spine, releasing your head from the top of your spine, and allowing your ribs to soften and your torso to be oriented back and up from your legs, take a wider stance with one step. Gently bend both knees while also recognizing that you are still keeping the floor away from you. Do not allow your pelvis to move forward with your knees and leave your feet flat on the floor as if your legs were still straight.

While pointing your spine, releasing your head, and allowing your ribs to soften and your torso to be oriented back and up from your legs, bend forward at the hip while recognizing that you are actually keeping your torso away from the floor. During and after the movement, notice that although your back is forward in space, it is oriented back and up in opposition to your legs which are going forward and down.

When you are ready to finish the exercise, as you gently press your heels into the floor until your legs straighten, **also rotate your torso back to vertical as if you were resisting a force behind you.** In one step, bring your feet together and just walk away. Be aware of your surroundings and leave the exercise until the next time.

Remain open to new discoveries every time you practice the exercise.	Don't rush. Give yourself plenty of time to repeat and understand each instruction.	Look for comfort by waiting for your muscles to soften, not through shifting.

Staying Back and Up As You Bend Forward

As your torso rotates forward, be sure you are bending from the hip, the lowest point from which the torso can bend. Leave your whole upper body the way it was before you started bending, with your whole torso widening, spine pointing, and head releasing from the top of your spine. Think of your torso as going up and back even as it rotates forward.

Head releasing from pointing spine.

Your back is going back and up.

Bending is still standing.

The knees go forward, the pelvis stays back.

Even as your knees bend, your legs still support you, reaching forward and down toward the floor.

Part VI, Section 6. Recognize the Dynamic Opposition

After practicing Parts I–V, while still leaning against the wall, your spine pointing, head releasing from the top of your spine, ribs softening, and continuing to develop all the previous conditions, bring your feet together and walk backwards until your heels touch the wall. As your feet walk backwards, be careful not to let your head drift back with them.

With your heels against the wall, recognize that although you are no longer leaning, your legs are still in opposition to your torso. Your legs are still going forward and down toward the floor and your whole torso, from the pelvis up, is still going back and up toward the wall.

Before and as you walk away from the wall, think of your whole torso, from your pelvis up, as continuing to be oriented up and back toward the wall as if the wall were coming with you. Walking away, allow your pelvis to be the last part of your torso touching the wall.

Take a few steps and stop with both feet underneath you. Avoid moving your feet around to settle; just stop. Without leaning back, recognize that your back is still oriented back and up in opposition to your legs which are going forward and down toward the floor. *Allow your torso to be light on your legs as if you were suspended above your legs. Allow your legs to hang from your torso.*

With one step, bring your feet together. As if your whole torso were still supported by the wall, gently send one knee forward until the heel comes up, send that heel back to the floor and repeat with the other knee, lifting each heel five times. Try to minimize the sway of your hips from side to side and avoid any forward movement of your pelvis. Recognize your hip joint at the junction between your legs and pelvis.

While pointing your spine, releasing your head from the top of your spine, and allowing your ribs to soften and your torso to be oriented back and up from your legs, take a wider stance with one step. Gently bend both knees while also recognizing that you are still keeping the floor away from you. Do not allow your pelvis to move forward with your knees and leave your feet flat on the floor as if your legs were still straight.

While pointing your spine, releasing your head, and allowing your ribs to soften and your torso to be oriented back and up from your legs, bend forward at the hip while recognizing that you are actually keeping your torso away from the floor. During and after the movement, notice that although your back is forward in space, it is oriented back and up in opposition to your legs which are going forward and down.

Remain here for a moment and look for the internal movement in that stillness. At each moment, your torso is rising above the floor even though it is not moving. Recognize that even though you are relatively still, your torso is still going up and away from the floor, and your legs are still extending down toward the floor in opposition to your torso.

When you are ready to finish the exercise, as you gently press your heels into the floor until your legs straighten, also rotate your torso back to vertical as if you were resisting a force behind you. In one step, bring your feet together and just walk away. Be aware of your surroundings and leave the exercise until the next time.

Remain open to new discoveries every time you practice the exercise.	Don't rush. Give yourself plenty of time to repeat and understand each instruction.	Look for comfort by waiting for your muscles to soften, not through shifting.

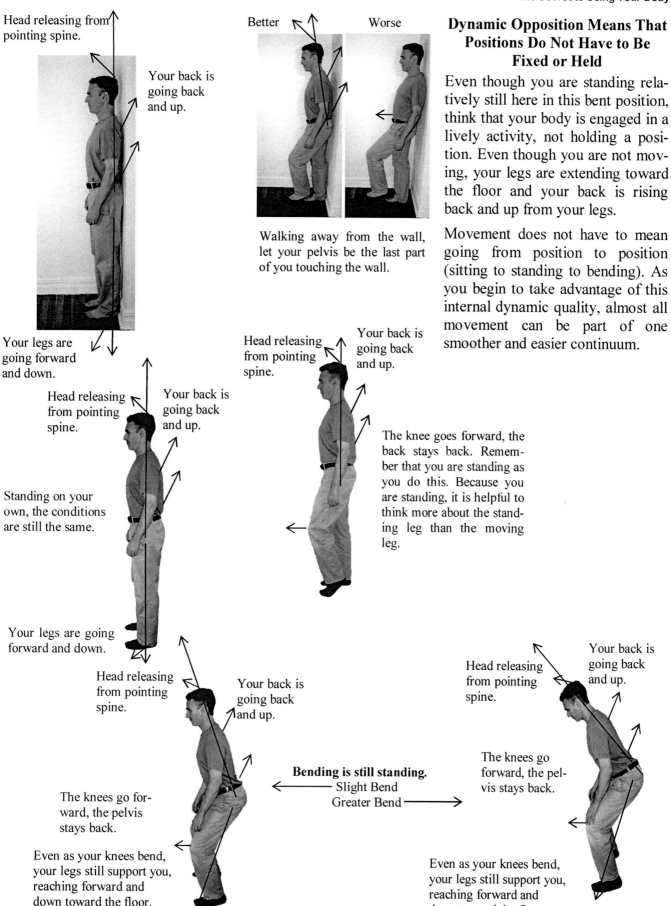

Head releasing from pointing spine.

Your back is going back and up.

Your legs are going forward and down.

Better   Worse

Walking away from the wall, let your pelvis be the last part of you touching the wall.

Head releasing from pointing spine.

Your back is going back and up.

Standing on your own, the conditions are still the same.

Your legs are going forward and down.

Head releasing from pointing spine.

Your back is going back and up.

The knees go forward, the pelvis stays back.

Even as your knees bend, your legs still support you, reaching forward and down toward the floor.

Bending is still standing.
⟵ Slight Bend
Greater Bend ⟶

Head releasing from pointing spine.

Your back is going back and up.

The knee goes forward, the back stays back. Remember that you are standing as you do this. Because you are standing, it is helpful to think more about the standing leg than the moving leg.

Head releasing from pointing spine.

Your back is going back and up.

The knees go forward, the pelvis stays back.

Even as your knees bend, your legs still support you, reaching forward and down toward the floor.

Dynamic Opposition Means That Positions Do Not Have to Be Fixed or Held

Even though you are standing relatively still here in this bent position, think that your body is engaged in a lively activity, not holding a position. Even though you are not moving, your legs are extending toward the floor and your back is rising back and up from your legs.

Movement does not have to mean going from position to position (sitting to standing to bending). As you begin to take advantage of this internal dynamic quality, almost all movement can be part of one smoother and easier continuum.

www.freeyourneck.com

Part VII

Application

Before You Begin

This seventh part of the exercise applies the instructions to activities that resemble things you do in your daily life, such as sitting, walking, and bending. It is the last formal part of the exercise and one of the last steps to prepare you to explore using your body with greater ease and strength.

The end of Part VI will leave you ready to begin the five sections of Part VII seamlessly while standing on your own. The activity for Part VII, virtually the same as all the previous parts of the exercise, is to discover the same conditions that you are establishing throughout the exercise as you stand, walk, and bend. Your objective is to avoid compromising your pointing spine, the release of your head from the top of your spine, your softening ribs, and all the work you are doing, for the sake of the movement. The movement is always secondary to allowing for room as you move.

Every time, before you practice Part VII, practice Parts I through VI first. Then spend 2–10 minutes on Part VII (more if you like) but remember that you do not need to lengthen the amount of time you spend on the whole exercise.

As you practice the exercise, you may discover a subtle difference in how you experience your body. Try to remain open to new discoveries every time. When you are ready to finish the exercise, just stop or walk away. Be aware of your surroundings and leave the exercise until the next time you practice it.

Equipment

A chair or stool of normal height with a firm seat for Sections 4 & 5.

Part VII, Section 1. Standing

After practicing Parts I–VI, while standing on your own, your spine pointing, head releasing from the top of your spine, ribs softening, and continuing to develop all the previous conditions:

- **Allow for the release of your head and ribs from your pointing spine.**

- **Gently point your shoulders away from each other as you allow for widening across your whole torso, front and back.**

- **As you allow your ankles to soften, imagine your legs lengthening from the bottom up.**

- **Allow your legs to release from your hip sockets. Think of your legs as hanging from your pelvis.**

- **Think of yourself as light and imagine your whole torso suspended above your legs.**

Standing still can become uncomfortable. Don't remain still for more than a minute before walking away. Be aware of your surroundings and leave the exercise until the next time.

Remain open to new discoveries every time you practice the exercise.	Don't rush. Give yourself plenty of time to repeat and understand each instruction.	Look for comfort by waiting for your muscles to soften, not through shifting.

Not Standing

First, remember that you are still just doing the exercise. This isn't how you are supposed to stand up.

Think of standing as something you have never done before. You are looking for something new so you have to look at this familiar activity in a new way. Avoid shuffling your feet or looking for the right position. Think of the exercise and practice it as if you were lying down. Allow your head and ribs to release from your pointing spine. Recognize your feet on the ground and give your body a moment to allow for openness. Look for the internal quality of movement, even though you are standing still.

Standing Free

When you are standing upright on your own, there is no longer a need to allow your back to fall back because there is nothing supporting it. Instead, try just to leave your back behind as you allow your head to release from your pointing spine. Avoid pushing your back forward or pulling your legs backward.

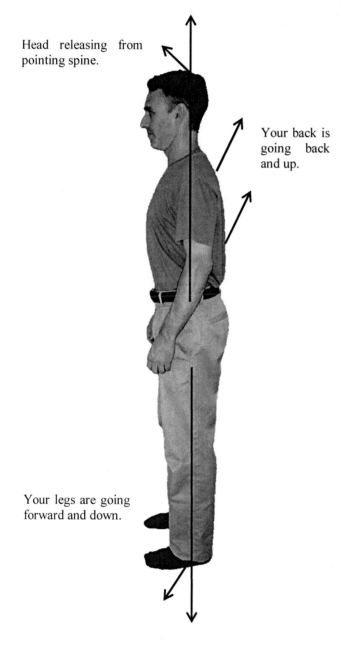

Standing on your own, the conditions are still the same.

Head releasing from pointing spine.

Your back is going back and up.

Your legs are going forward and down.

www.freeyourneck.com

Part VII, Section 2. Walking

After practicing Parts I–VI, while standing on your own, your spine pointing, head releasing from the top of your spine, ribs softening, and continuing to develop all the previous conditions:

- Allow for the release of your head and ribs from your pointing spine.

- Gently point your shoulders away from each other as you allow for widening across your whole torso, front and back.

- As you allow your ankles to soften, imagine your legs lengthening from the bottom up.

- Allow your legs to release from your hip sockets. Think of your legs as hanging from your pelvis.

- Think of yourself as light and imagine your whole torso suspended above your legs.

- **Continuing to release your head and ribs from your pointing spine, send one knee forward and then the other as you walk normally. Your nose and knee lead, your whole torso stays behind your head and pelvis. Think of yourself as light above your legs.**

- **When you are ready to finish the exercise, just stop thinking about it and walk away.** Be aware of your surroundings and leave the exercise until the next time.

Remain open to new discoveries every time you practice the exercise.	Don't rush. Give yourself plenty of time to repeat and understand each instruction.	Look for comfort by waiting for your muscles to soften, not through shifting.

Not Walking

You do this while lying down in Part II. Take walking out of context and avoid thinking that you are going somewhere or even that you are walking. You are just moving one knee forward and then the other while pointing your spine and releasing your head and ribs. Avoid allowing your neck or pelvis to get in front of you.

If It Feels Strange

It is common to feel strange when you do something familiar in a new way. Don't worry.

Walking

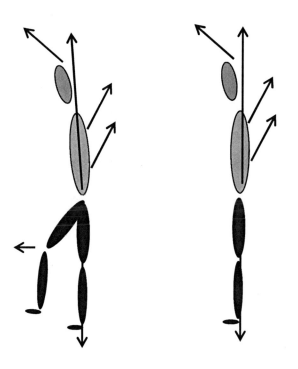

Even as you keep sending your knees forward, leave your pelvis behind your legs and your neck behind your head.

Remember that while you are moving forward, you are also standing, staying up above the ground.

Part VII, Section 3. Touch the Floor

- After practicing Parts I–VI, while standing on your own, your spine pointing, head releasing from the top of your spine, ribs softening, and continuing to develop all the previous conditions:

- Allow for the release of your head and ribs from your pointing spine.

- Gently point your shoulders away from each other as you allow for widening across your whole torso, front and back.

- As you allow your ankles to soften, imagine your legs lengthening from the bottom up.

- Allow your legs to release from your hip sockets. Think of your legs as hanging from your pelvis.

- Think of yourself as light and imagine your whole torso suspended above your legs.

- Continuing to release your head and ribs from your pointing spine, send one knee forward and then the other as you walk normally. Your nose and knee lead, your whole torso stays behind your head and pelvis. Think of yourself as light above your legs.

- **Continuing to release your head and ribs from your pointing spine, stop walking and take a wide stance with one step.**

- **Without lifting your ribs or pulling on your head, imagine your torso suspended above your legs as you point your spine and release your legs from your hip sockets.**

- **Leaving your feet on the floor as if you were standing, send your knees forward, while leaving your pelvis behind, as your whole torso also rotates forward.**

- **Bend only as far as you can maintain the conditions.**

- **Send your feet into the floor to stand up.**

- **Walk away when you are finished with the exercise. Be aware of your surroundings and leave the exercise until the next time.**

Remain open to new discoveries every time you practice the exercise.	Don't rush. Give yourself plenty of time to repeat and understand each instruction.	Look for comfort by waiting for your muscles to soften, not through shifting.

Moving Down and Forward While Staying Back and Up

As you bend, observe your torso and your head/neck relationship staying the same as if you were not bending. Observe yourself leaving your feet completely on the floor and imagining your whole torso going up as you move down. Avoid thinking that you are touching the floor. Notice that as long as your feet are fully on the floor, you will feel more stable.

People often tell me that they feel like a puppet when they do movements like these. I answer by telling them that for the first time they are now holding the strings.

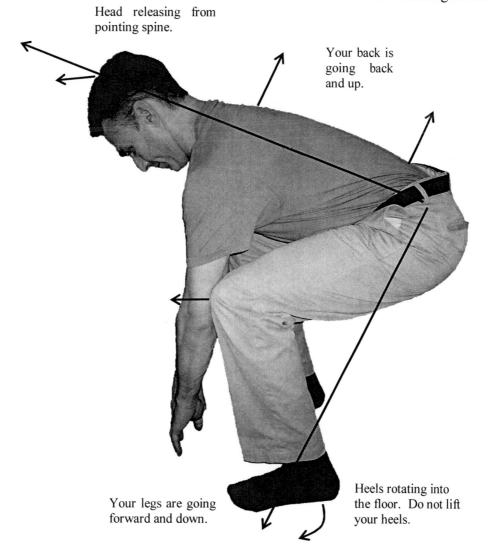

Head releasing from pointing spine.

Your back is going back and up.

Your legs are going forward and down.

Heels rotating into the floor. Do not lift your heels.

www.freeyourneck.com

Part VII, Section 4. Using A Chair: Sitting and Standing

After practicing Parts I–VI, while standing on your own, your spine pointing, head releasing from the top of your spine, ribs softening, and continuing to develop all the previous conditions:

- Allow for the release of your head and ribs from your pointing spine.

- Gently point your shoulders away from each other as you allow for widening across your whole torso, front and back.

- As you allow your ankles to soften, imagine your legs lengthening from the bottom up.

- Allow your legs to release from your hip sockets. Think of your legs as hanging from your pelvis.

- Think of yourself as light and imagine your whole torso suspended above your legs.

- Continuing to release your head and ribs from your pointing spine, send one knee forward and then the other as you walk normally. Your nose and knee lead, your whole torso stays behind your head and pelvis. Think of yourself as light above your legs.

- Continuing to release your head and ribs from your pointing spine, stop walking and take a wide stance with one step.

- Without lifting your ribs or pulling on your head, imagine your torso suspended above your legs as you point your spine and release your legs from your hip sockets.

- Leaving your feet on the floor as if you were standing, send your knees forward, while leaving your pelvis behind, as your whole torso also rotates forward.

- Bend only as far as you can maintain the conditions.

- Send your feet into the floor to stand up.

- **Stand in front of a chair. Repeat Section 3 with a narrower stance. Do not compromise your activity for the sake of the chair. When arriving at the chair, do not settle in the chair or tilt the torso back. Just send your feet into the floor and stand up.**

- Walk away when you are finished with the exercise. Be aware of your surroundings and leave the exercise until the next time.

Remain open to new discoveries every time you practice the exercise.	Don't rush. Give yourself plenty of time to repeat and understand each instruction.	Look for comfort by waiting for your muscles to soften, not through shifting.

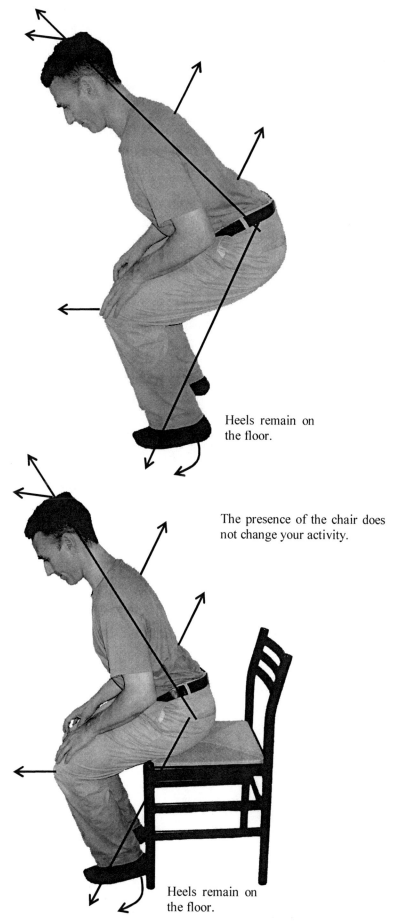

Heels remain on the floor.

The presence of the chair does not change your activity.

Heels remain on the floor.

Sitting and Not Sitting

The movement that leaves you sitting in a chair or standing from a seated position is very similar to the movement that ends with you touching the floor. The only difference is the horizontal platform (the chair) that blocks your progression toward the floor. As you do this section, keep your mind on observing your pointing spine and the rest of the instructions. Standing in front of the chair, imagine that the chair isn't there. The chair is simply a horizontal plane that gets in your way as you bend your knees. As you bend, always leave your feet flat on the floor and avoid falling into the chair. Once you reach the chair, send your heels into the floor and come right up again.

Does This Look Weird?

The short answer is "no." It might feel weird because it is a new way to do a familiar thing. But remember, you arc just doing an exercise here.

Part VII, Section 5. Full Exercise

After practicing Parts I–VI, while standing on your own, your spine pointing, head releasing from the top of your spine, ribs softening, and continuing to develop all the previous conditions:

- Allow for the release of your head and ribs from your pointing spine.

- Gently point your shoulders away from each other as you allow for widening across your whole torso, front and back.

- As you allow your ankles to soften, imagine your legs lengthening from the bottom up.

- Allow your legs to release from your hip sockets. Think of your legs as hanging from your pelvis.

- Think of yourself as light and imagine your whole torso suspended above your legs.

- Continuing to release your head and ribs from your pointing spine, send one knee forward and then the other as you walk normally. Your nose and knee lead, your whole torso stays behind your head and pelvis. Think of yourself as light above your legs.

- Continuing to release your head and ribs from your pointing spine, stop walking and take a wide stance with one step.

- Without lifting your ribs or pulling on your head, imagine your torso suspended above your legs as you point your spine and release your legs from your hip sockets.

- Leaving your feet on the floor as if you were standing, send your knees forward, while leaving your pelvis behind, as your whole torso also rotates forward.

- Bend only as far as you can maintain the conditions.

- Send your feet into the floor to stand up.

- Stand in front of a chair. Repeat Section 3 with a narrower stance. Do not compromise your activity for the sake of the chair. When arriving at the chair, do not settle in the chair or tilt the torso back. Just send your feet into the floor and stand up.

- Walk away when you are finished with the exercise. Be aware of your surroundings and leave the exercise until the next time.

Remain open to new discoveries every time you practice the exercise.	Don't rush. Give yourself plenty of time to repeat and understand each instruction.	Look for comfort by waiting for your muscles to soften, not through shifting.

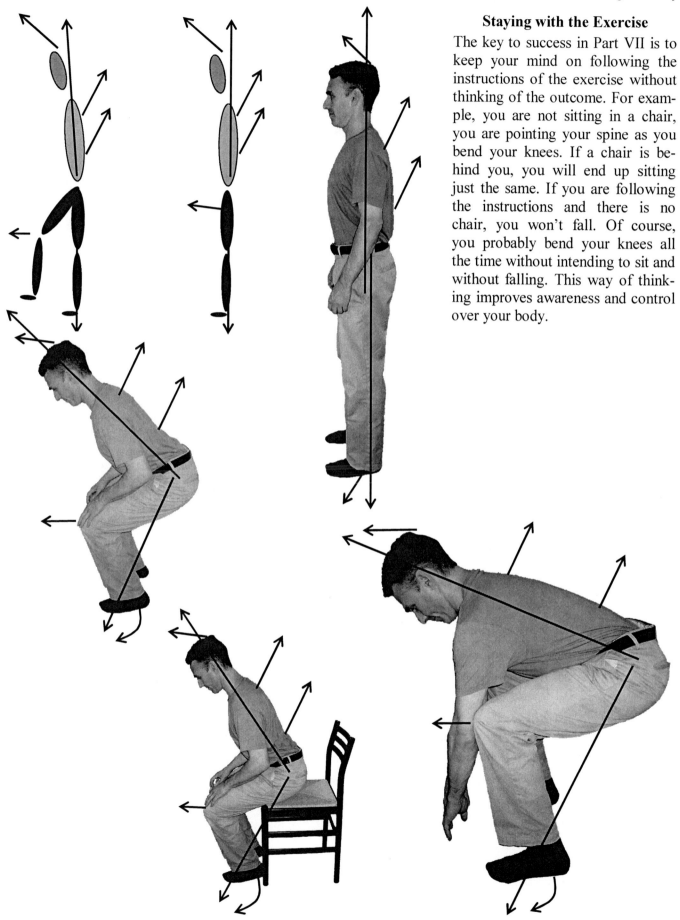

Staying with the Exercise

The key to success in Part VII is to keep your mind on following the instructions of the exercise without thinking of the outcome. For example, you are not sitting in a chair, you are pointing your spine as you bend your knees. If a chair is behind you, you will end up sitting just the same. If you are following the instructions and there is no chair, you won't fall. Of course, you probably bend your knees all the time without intending to sit and without falling. This way of thinking improves awareness and control over your body.

Part VIII

Mindfulness & Using the Whole Exercise

Until now you have been using the exercise to introduce yourself to the concepts of the Alexander Technique. Now that you have learned the exercise, continue using it to develop your skills. Besides the nuts and bolts of each section, there are two overriding concepts that are important to fully understand and trust.

The first of these concepts is that the whole exercise is a meditation on mindful patience. It asks you, over and over, to focus on and complete almost imperceptible subtle actions. Your posture is the product of the ways you habitually move and hold your body. To change and improve those habits you will have to give yourself time to experience what you are doing and allow yourself to do something else, like release your head and ribs from your pointing spine. In fact, your willingness to mindfully and non-judgmentally observe yourself and make the new choices that are suggested in the exercise is more important than actually succeeding at following the instructions. All that is required is that you give yourself time to try.

The second concept is recognizing the generic quality of proper movement and body use. The exercise is purposefully repetitive. As an Alexander teacher, one of the most frequent questions my students ask me is how some specific task can be done in an Alexander way. The short answer to this is something that you might guess: by releasing your head and ribs from your pointing spine (and all the rest). Although you may not understand how to actualize the instructions, as you prepare to use your new skills in your daily life, it is important to realize that the instructions are almost always a valid choice for any movement. As you begin to understand and trust the ideas that run through the exercise, you will begin to make them your own and the way you use your body will change.

As you practice the exercise, don't be overly concerned with getting it right. Instead, in order to develop your non-judgmental mindfulness, **observe yourself establishing the conditions as you practice the exercise.** In other words, as you practice, say to yourself, for example, "now I am releasing my head and ribs from my pointing spine as I bend my knees." Remember that the movement is always secondary to establishing and maintaining the conditions even if you are imperfect at establishing the conditions. In addition to your mindful observation, **be sure to pay attention to the similarities from section to section.** Understanding that similarity is one of the keys to understanding and benefiting from the Alexander Technique.

Use the exercise for as long as it takes until it consistently feels physically comfortable before you begin experimenting with your posture in your daily life. As your familiarity with the exercise increases, feel free to change the order or to work on the exercise in parts. Use it when you are waiting in line or sitting in a chair. Always keep your eyes open and remain aware of your surroundings. Part I especially can be done in any order and, for example, the whole exercise can be done backwards. Changing the exercise will help you to better understand it. You can also add Auxiliary Exercises I and II from the pages that follow as you see fit. Try to use the exercise every day, but also remember to enjoy playing with it.

Auxiliary Exercise I
Sitting in a Chair

Before You Begin

Auxiliary Exercise I helps you discover greater comfort while sitting in a chair and is not included in the formal exercise. Once you learn it, it can be used whenever you find yourself sitting in a chair and you have a couple of minutes or are feeling uncomfortable. You can do it at work or while sitting in a waiting room or any other time you want to feel more comfortable. Of course you can also go and sit in a chair in order to practice, but if you are already sitting, you are ready to begin. It is also the first part of the exercise that is written specifically for integration into your daily life. It uses all the same concepts of the exercise, except in a seated position. The activity for this exercise is to **develop the same conditions that you are establishing throughout the exercise as you sit in the chair.**

Equipment

A chair or stool of normal height with a firm seat.

 www.freeyourneck.com

Auxiliary Exercise I

Sitting in a Chair

Once you are sitting in a chair, neither freeze in place nor change position. Think of what you know from the exercise but don't jump into an exercise mode. Work slowly in an organic way, not by jumping into position (which doesn't improve anything).

Think of sitting as if the chair had replaced your legs and that you are actually standing on the chair as if it were your legs.

Allow the lowest part of your sit bones to sink into the chair.

Place your attention on the back of your neck and the area just below the base of your skull and allow it to soften. This is the same as allowing the head to release from the top of your spine.

Gently point your spine.

Allow for space between your torso and your legs.

Allow your heels to drift toward the floor. Your heels can be off the floor so long as you are not pulling them off the floor. Let your feet and legs fall into the floor. If your legs are crossed, you'll only have one foot connected to the floor, which is fine as long as you are comfortable.

As you move your upper body avoid unnecessarily pulling on your legs and feet. Pulling your legs toward you makes you smaller and tends to pull you off the chair.

To maintain comfort, get up or change positions often. The body gets uncomfortable when it stays in one position. As you move, avoid unnecessarily pulling your head into your neck.

To get out of the chair, rotate your torso forward until you have weight over your feet. Continue pointing your spine and avoid pulling your torso in front of your head in order to get out of the chair.

Remain open to new discoveries every time you practice the exercise.	Don't rush. Give yourself plenty of time to repeat and understand each instruction.	Look for comfort by waiting for your muscles to soften, not through shifting.

Better

Worse

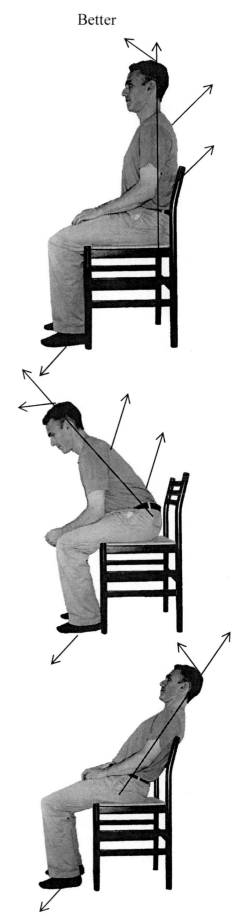

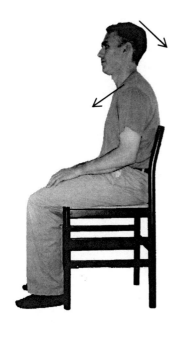

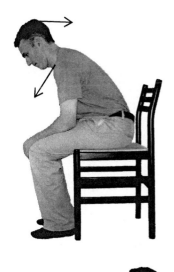

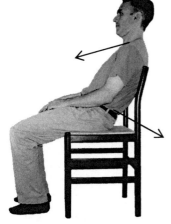

Auxiliary Exercise II

Common Movements

The instructions for the Alexander Technique work in any position and for any movement, such as looking up, reaching, turning, and so on. The following images and explanations are not part of the exercise, but you can incorporate them into the exercise if you wish.

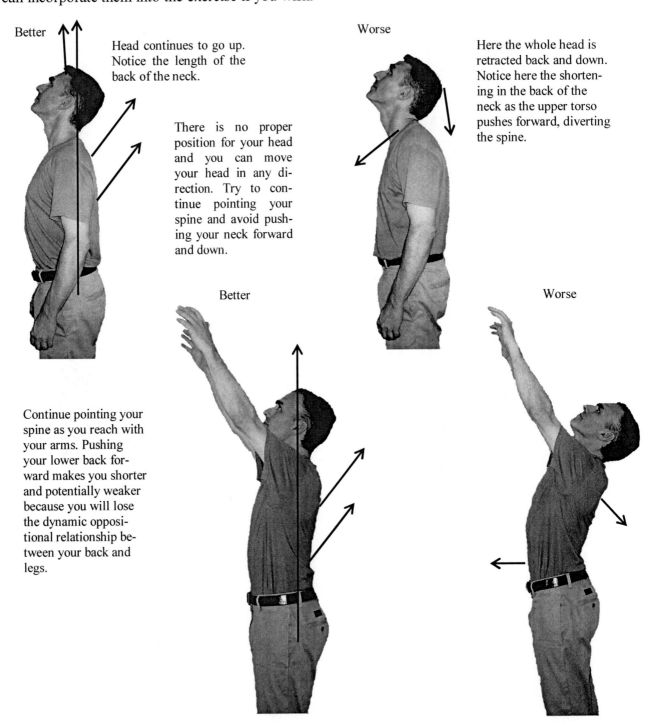

Better

Head continues to go up. Notice the length of the back of the neck.

There is no proper position for your head and you can move your head in any direction. Try to continue pointing your spine and avoid pushing your neck forward and down.

Worse

Here the whole head is retracted back and down. Notice here the shortening in the back of the neck as the upper torso pushes forward, diverting the spine.

Better

Worse

Continue pointing your spine as you reach with your arms. Pushing your lower back forward makes you shorter and potentially weaker because you will lose the dynamic oppositional relationship between your back and legs.

Remain open to new discoveries every time you practice the exercise.	Don't rush. Give yourself plenty of time to repeat and understand each instruction.	Look for comfort by waiting for your muscles to soften, not through shifting.

Even in twisting, the spine can still point and you can still establish a dynamic oppositional relationship between your torso and legs.

The lunge is a common athletic movement. Here you rely on one leg to establish a dynamic oppositional relationship between the leg and torso.

Part IX

Bringing Your Awareness into Your Daily Life

Before You Begin

If the exercise feels comfortable, you may be ready to begin transferring what you have learned to your daily life. There are different ways that you can pursue this, and one or all of the following methods may be suitable for you. Choosing a method depends on your goal for reading this book, your temperament, how well the exercise is working, and the situation to which you are applying it.

Basic Transfer

You may only be concerned with bending and lifting more safely. You can specifically practice these and other common movements described in the exercise and transfer them directly. The more you use these new movements, the more normal they will become.

Organic Transfer

The way people use their body tends to feel normal to them. The exercise is designed to help you improve the way you move and stand and to make that new way feel normal. If this aspect of the exercise is working for you, and you have been doing the exercise long enough and consistently enough, you may have already found that the way you use your body has improved. It may even continue to improve in this way, especially if you continue to do the exercise or to think about the exercise in your daily life. It is also possible that you have made progress without noticing because the change now seems normal. Sometimes other people will notice a change in you before you notice it in yourself.

System Transfer

The exercise also teaches you a system that you can use to improve the way you use your body in your regular life. In using the system, you consciously seek to establish the conditions developed in the exercise in your regular life. To use this method, just as in the exercise, the establishment of the conditions must be more important than the completion of the movement or the task at hand. In the System Transfer method, the Alexander Technique becomes a tool for solving problems of movement. Obviously you can't do this in an emergency, but most days have many opportunities for taking advantage of your new skills. The more you think about establishing the conditions of an open body in your daily life, the more this new way of using your body will become normal for you while your old way becomes uncomfortable.

Self Observation Transfer

As we meet the challenges of our daily lives (whether they are related to movement like lifting or getting up from a chair, or from the psychological realm such as how we respond to people, including ourselves, and situations) often our first response is a subtle tightening of the neck, pulling the head back and down toward the spine. People even comment on how a stressful day will make their neck hurt. Through using the exercise, you may have become adept at noticing and avoiding the tendency to tighten your neck. By noticing how you respond to a given situation and allowing for a more open body through your new awareness, you will continue to transfer and build upon your skills, improving your posture and movement, while also projecting a more measured and thoughtful demeanor.

Choice

No matter how you incorporate what you have learned, the Alexander Technique is about giving you more than the one way you formerly had for using your body. Do not feel that you have to hold your body or move in a certain way. This will only cause discomfort and possibly pain.

Use your awareness easily and avoid forcing yourself. Look at your efforts as an experiment and return to the book if you need to re-evaluate how you are using your new skills.

Part X

Moving Forward

This book has asked you to examine and change some of your most intimate habits, like the tightness of your neck, and the ease of your rib movement. Moment by moment, these habits are among the smallest, least impactful actions that we do. But because they are intrinsic to the fabric of our lives, taken together, they amount to how we behave and what we do. They are what we are. When you reduce the amount you tighten your neck or torso in response to a situation, you change the way you respond to that situation. If you have recognized and changed some of these habits, even marginally, you have changed yourself and you have proven that change and growth are possible for you.

I tell this story to most of my students: One day I drove my elderly aunt from Queens to her doctor in Manhattan. During her appointment I listened to the radio in the car. What I didn't realize was that the lights were also on, and the battery died a few minutes before my aunt emerged from the office. Thinking of the trouble my foolish action would cause for my aunt, I became very anxious and upset. I could feel myself collapsing as I started to put my head in my hands. But then I also remembered the Alexander Technique and that I wouldn't solve my problem by drawing myself inward. I allowed my body to open and I looked around. There, right next to me, was a tow truck stopped at a red light. I spoke to the driver, he pulled jumper cables from the side of his truck, and my car was running within two minutes of my realizing what had happened.

I have called this book *The Secret to Using Your Body: A Manual for Looking Better and Feeling Younger with the Alexander Technique.* I hope that the exercise you have learned not only addresses how to stand taller and move more easily, but also gives you a tool to see yourself, and your secrets, more clearly. I hope it continues to help you make better choices and seek new answers.

Remain open to new discoveries every time you practice the exercise.	Don't rush. Give yourself plenty of time to repeat and understand each instruction.	Look for comfort by waiting for your muscles to soften, not through shifting.

Resources

To contact Leland Vall to schedule an Alexander Technique lesson or demonstration, and to find videos and articles on the Alexander Technique, visit **www.freeyourneck.com**.

To find an Alexander Technique teacher in your area, contact the American Society for the Alexander Technique at **www.amsat.ws**.

Selected Bibliography

Alexander, F. M. *Articles and Lectures.* London: Mouritz, 1995.

Alexander, F. M. *Constructive Conscious Control of the Individual.* New York: E. P. Dutton & Co., 1923.

Alexander, F. M. *Man's Supreme Inheritance.* Long Beach: Centerline Press, 1988.

Alexander, F. M. *The Universal Constant in Living.* New York: E. P. Dutton & Co., 1941.

Alexander, F. M. *The Use of the Self.* New York: E. P. Dutton & Co., 1932.

Barlow, Wilfred. *More Talk of Alexander.* London: Victor Gollancz LTD, 1978.

Conable, Barbara & William Conable. *How to Learn the Alexander Technique.* Portland: Andover Press, 1995.

de Alcantara, Pedro. *The Alexander Technique: A Skill for Life.* Wiltshire: The Crowood Press, 1999.

de Alcantara, Pedro. *Indirect Procedures: A Musician's Guide to the Alexander Technique.* New York: Oxford University Press, 1997.

Gelb, Michael J. *Body Learning.* New York: Henry Holt & Co., 1994.

Jones, Frank Pierce. *Body Awareness in Action.* New York: Schocken Books, 1979.

Leibowitz, Judith & Bill Connington. *The Alexander Technique.* New York: Harper Perennial, 1991.

Masterton, Alisa. *Alexander Technique: A Step-By-Step Guide.* Boston: Element Books, 1998.

Stough, Carl & Reece Stough. *Dr. Breath: The Story of Breathing Coordination.* New York: The Stough Institute, 1981.

Vineyard, Missy. *How You Stand, How You Move, How You Live.* New York: Marlowe & Co., 2007.

Westfeldt, Lulie. *F. Matthias Alexander: The Man and His Work.* London: Mouritz, 1998.

Acknowledgments

I am grateful to the following people for their help with this project: my teachers, Ruth Kilroy, Rivka Cohen, Hope Gillerman, Jessica Wolf, and the late Saura Bartner; Louis Colaianni, for encouraging me to start; John Boyd and the Chelsea Piers Sports Center where I taught over 200 drop-in group Alexander classes that helped me develop much of the material for this manual; all of my students, especially Tom Clayman, Emily Garrick, Mark Bower, Mark Dichter, Susan Gill, David Knee, Doreen Grosso, Nadine McCarthy, and Steve Mason; and finally, my colleagues and friends, Margaret Vetare, Glenn Kenreich, Rebecca Tuffey, and Honor Merceret.

About the Author

Leland Vall received his undergraduate degree from Hampshire College and studied theatrical directing at Trinity Repertory Conservatory with Anne Bogart. He had his first Alexander Technique lesson in 1982 and has been certified to teach the Alexander Technique since 1996. He received his training and certification at the Alexander Technique Training Center in Boston, directed by Ruth Kilroy. He has a private practice in Manhattan, Queens, and Long Island, and has also taught the Alexander Technique at Chelsea Piers Sports Center, Crunch Fitness, American Academy of Dramatic Arts, and the School for Film and Television. His students range from healthy people who want to look and feel better, to athletes and performing artists interested in improving performance, to others managing chronic pain, illness, or injury recovery.

Certification to teach the Alexander Technique requires the completion of three years of training. Mr. Vall is certified to teach the Alexander Technique by the American Society for the Alexander Technique (AmSAT), the largest organization of its kind in the United States. He has a special certification in The Art of Breathing from the American Center for the Alexander Technique (ACAT), and a personal trainer certification from the American Council on Exercise (ACE).

Leland Vall is a former board member of the American Center for the Alexander Technique, the oldest Alexander training facility in the country, and he is a former editor of the *AmSAT News*, the official newsletter of the American Society for the Alexander Technique.

CPSIA information can be obtained at www.ICGtesting.com
Printed in the USA
LVOW021939200911

247099LV00003B/7/P